Scientific Reading Assessment
Targeted Intervention and Follow-Up Lessons

Maryann Manning

Shelly Chumley

Clark Underbakke

HEINEMANN
Portsmouth, NH

Heinemann
A division of Reed Elsevier Inc.
361 Hanover Street
Portsmouth, NH 03801–3912
www.heinemann.com

Offices and agents throughout the world

Library of Congress Cataloging-in-Publication Data
Manning, Maryann Murphy.
    Scientific reading assessment : targeted intervention and follow-up lessons /
Maryann Manning, Shelly Chumley, Clark Underbakke.
        p.   cm.
    Includes bibliographical references and index.
    ISBN-13: 978-0-325-00835-6
    ISBN-10: 0-325-00835-3
    1. Reading (Elementary)—United States.   2. Reading (Elementary)—United
States—Evaluation.   I. Chumley, Shelly.   II. Underbakke, Clark.   III. Title.
    LB1573.M333 2006
    372.48—dc22   2006010218

Editor: Lois Bridges
Production coordinator: Elizabeth Valway
Production service: Denise A. Botelho
Cover design: Gina Poirier
Cover photographs: Clark Underbakke
Composition: Publishers' Design and Production Services, Inc.
Manufacturing: Steve Bernier

Printed in the United States of America on acid-free paper
10 09 08 07 06 ML 1 2 3 4 5

Contents

Dedication

Through the years, we have had the privilege of watching many young children learn to read. These children encompass those we have taught and worked with as well as those we have known intimately, and from afar. We thrive on watching literacy develop. Five children in particular are special to us: Artie and Marilee Manning, Mary Claire and Emma Grace Chumley, and Emily Hagood. One remains with us only in spirit, another has matured into a fine young woman, whereas the other three still enjoy the carefree lives of children. To these five children, from whom we have learned the most about learning how to read, we dedicate this book.

Artie and Marilee Manning

During their childhoods and even into their young adulthoods, Maryann's children, Artie and Marilee, were absolute opposites. Artie was a very bright boy with cerebral palsy before his untimely death at age 26 when he was a teacher of special education. Artie didn't really begin reading or writing until he was ten years old. At this time, he found his own Annie Sullivan in Barbara Lewis, the teacher who helped him become literate. Artie was never considered a truly fluent reader or writer. Undaunted, this did not stop him from earning Bachelor of Science and Master's degrees in education.

On the other hand, Marilee was an early reader and writer who progressed quickly through all the stages of literacy without difficulty. Marilee enjoyed every aspect of school and learning. Marilee graduated Phi Beta Kappa from the University of Texas and UT School of Law and currently resides on Long Island with her husband Lance. While awaiting the arrival of her first child, she is working on a PhD in child advocacy.

Mary Claire and Emma Grace

Shelly, along with husband Phillip, finds herself raising two voracious readers. None of us will forget Mary Claire's learning to read before the age of four. As we finish this book, she is in third grade and is author Richard Peck's biggest fan. Recently, we were at Shelly and Phillip's for dinner and watched in delight as Emma Grace read unfamiliar, simple text without assistance, proudly showing the illustrations "just like a teacher." Having just turned three as we finish this manuscript, her favorite books include *Going on a Bear Hunt* by Helen Oxenbury and *Time for Bed* by Mem Fox.

Emily

Emily Hagood is the daughter of our friends, Toni Shay and William Hagood. At her fourth birthday celebration, we witnessed Emily open her birthday cards and read each one aloud. Having both parents involved in educational publishing and being surrounded by consummate educators fills Emily's life with rich literacy episodes and constant oral and written language interactions.

Foreword

Being approached to write a foreword for a new book from Heinemann was both an honor and a challenge. Having met Maryann years ago at various literacy conferences and having read her previous work, I knew that she and her colleagues would put together a quality resource that would be both enjoyable to read and supportive of teachers' instructional decisions. However, when I heard the book was about reading assessment, I will be honest: I was reluctant to take on the responsibility for writing the foreword and promoting another book on assessment. Thankfully, this book is about much more.

Scientific Reading Assessment: Targeted Intervention and Follow-Up Lessons is about keeping assessment in its proper place and using it more efficiently to learn and guide instruction. This book also demonstrates how reading assessments can be used to provide quality instruction at the point of students' needs, leading to more proficient and successful readers.

In today's political climate, it's hard to find a politician who doesn't use educational reform or teacher accountability in campaign rhetoric. It doesn't take long, however, to figure out what these politicians are really referring to is the need to raise standardized test scores, and teachers' responsibility in doing so. Unfortunately, relying on a single test score to present an accurate portrayal of a particular classroom, school, district, or geographic region is like determining the quality of a hospital's care by calculating the average body temperature of its patients. It gives you a number all right, but it doesn't mean that much.

Standardized test scores give the public a false sense of security that schools, teachers, and students are doing well, and a false sense of accountability about which schools are falling behind. The reading assessments that teachers draw on must go beyond single test scores. Teachers need multifaceted, in-depth information that they can use to target their intervention and shape their instruction.

In schools across America today, we are conducting far too much externally mandated assessment and far too little classroom-based assessment. Classroom teachers are busy people, very busy. They need *real* scientific assessments that give them the "biggest bang for the buck." In other words, teachers need efficient assessments that provide them with the types of information that help them teach better. Teachers should not have to gather information that they are not able to reflect on and use to inform their teaching.

This book begins by providing assessment resources to help teachers know their students as readers. But it goes a step beyond simply being a book about assessment. *Scientific Reading Assessment* provides teachers with the help they need to interpret these assessments and use the information generated to give students the essential instructional experiences they need to take their next learning steps.

Part I provides an overview of the authors' theoretical foundation. Maryann, Shelly, and Clark lay out their definition of reading and the reading process, and provide readers with insights into why they do what they do in the name of reading instruction. Included in this opening section is a list of "nonnegotiables" related to literacy instruction. This list, and its accompanying set of belief statements, lays out for the reader the theoretical underpinnings of the book, and sets the tone for the upcoming chapters.

Part II takes you on a quick tour of various reading assessments and gives the reader numerous references and sources of information about reading assessment to delve further into if so desired. The assessment section focuses on the multiple sources of information that teachers draw upon to come to know their students as readers and ways to tap these sources efficiently, without taking valuable time away from instruction.

Part III explores the connections between the assessments teachers use to understand readers' processes and abilities, and the lessons that support readers' development. Each of the lessons the authors present begins with a brief explanation of the classroom observations that led to the enactment of the lesson to come. Supporting Yetta Goodman's notion of *kidwatching* the authors provide short vignettes focusing on students' language and classroom experiences that would suggest the need for a particular lesson. They provide a brief rationale for each lesson and then give examples of how the lesson might proceed.

Supporting a "Gradual Release of Responsibility Model," each lesson concludes with suggestions for helping readers take on the strategies and practices demonstrated in the lesson and assume responsibility for what was taught. Unfortunately, the lessons included in many teaching resources conclude with what the teacher should do, not with what the student is expected to do. The focus remains on teaching, not on the learning that is expected. *Scientific Read-*

ing Assessment helps teachers bridge the gap between teaching and learning by including expectations and suggestions for what should take place in the classroom once the lesson is concluded. The carefully selected vignettes and portrayals of actual readers help illuminate the classroom environments and allow the reader a window into the instructional space recommended by the authors.

Another unique aspect of *Scientific Reading Assessment* is the series of letters to parents and caregivers that are included with many of the lessons. What a wonderful idea! Extending instructional practices and reading strategies into the homes of our students helps support readers both in and out of school, and gives parents and caregivers ideas for working with their children at home. Too often our instruction ends at the classroom door. The letters included with the lessons offer suggestions and resources for supporting readers when they leave our instructional space behind.

The lessons included in *Scientific Reading Assessment* keep the focus on the construction and negotiation of meaning. The variety of lessons presented in the book covers a wide range of topics, texts, and reading strategies. Teachers will find this book to be a valuable resource as they make connections between reading assessments and instructional opportunities. I expect to see dog-eared copies of this book on many classroom teachers' desks for years to come.

Frank Serafini

Preface

So many distractions waste our time when we are busy teaching. The cry we hear from so many teachers is, "I don't have time for all this paperwork!" or "If I'm given one more test to give, I'm going to have a breakdown right this minute!" Well-meaning politicians and administrators add to our job requirements by mandating more testing, more documentation, and more seemingly meaningless paperwork. Each of these additional responsibilities robs us of precious time to do what we know must be done in our classrooms . . . *teach*.

When we speak out against standardized testing, we are often accused of not wanting to be accountable. Nothing could be further from the truth because we know that to have good teaching, assessment and accountability are necessary. But we want the assessments we use to inform us about instruction and guide our teaching. We do not want assessment merely to be a reduced group of numbers on a printout that purports to represent everything our students know. Nor do we want our worth or value as teachers to be determined by how well our children perform on standardized tests. Assessment should be genuine and should involve authentic reading and writing. Simply filling in the circle marked a, b, c, or d, or chopping up words into little pieces isn't what assessment looks like to us.

The teaching of reading should be grounded in quality children's literature, and family members and caregivers should be invited to extend learning in the home. We have endeavored to cut your preparation time by identifying many of the common needs of readers that we see in our own, as well as in other teachers', classrooms. We have developed lessons that you can use quickly and concisely. Many of the lessons incorporate pieces of well-known, readily available children's literature. Others include reproducible pages for you to use with your class be it individually, in small groups, or with the whole class. Each lesson includes ways to involve family members and care-givers in the process of learning to read.

It is our hope that this book will simplify your life and give you a few extra minutes each day. We hope that your students will find the lessons inter-esting and that the experiences will refine them as readers.

Acknowledgments

Together, we thank the many teachers with whom we have worked and the colleagues with whom we have learned much from over the years. Tsuguhiko Kato and Emily Treadwell were helpful to us with editing our writing and locating our references. We thank Denise Botelho, our project coordinator, who answered our many questions and guided us through editing our manuscript with countless emails and a helpful ear. Especially warm thanks to Lois Bridges, our editor, who had confidence in our ideas, provided encouragement throughout the development of the manuscript, and soothed the nerves of two novice and one experienced author.

Introduction

For better or worse, assessment drives instruction. As teachers, we are all faced with this often-challenging reality. Testing permeates the lives of teachers and students across grade levels and content areas. The assessment of reading has been at the forefront of discussion among teachers, researchers, administrators, policymakers, and politicians.

During the past several years, we have seen an abundance of assessment materials enter the marketplace. Each promises a new and improved way to analyze our students. Some purport to be "research based," whereas others offer a quick yet comprehensive reader analysis. Individual schools, school systems, and some states have implemented reading assessment. Reading specialists and coaches abound in schools, ensuring that assessments are completed in compliance with predetermined standards.

Federal, state, and local governments expend resources to assess students. Teachers spend scarce classroom time preparing for and administering assessments. In our experience, however, teachers are not readily able to take advantage of the information the assessments yield.

Maryann is a university professor teaching hundreds of undergraduate and graduate students each year. Through her travels and dedication to literacy education, she interacts with teachers and students in their classrooms across our nation and around the world. She often hears teachers lament over assessment. Shelly has taught grades 6, 5, and 2. At the moment, she works with many teachers as a reading coach. The teachers at her kindergarten-through-grade 5 school are often frustrated by the vast amounts of assessment required of them and their students. Clark has taught grades 5, 4, and 2. Currently, he teaches second grade.

All of us have felt the pressure of assessment. We have felt as though we spend more time assessing our students than teaching them. We have all endured assessments imposed at all levels. We have often sat together with friends and colleagues discussing the merits and pitfalls of assessment. We wonder what assessments tell us and what we should do with the information yielded. We wonder whether the assessments are useful and, if so, whether we are maximizing their usefulness. Clearly, we all recognize that many teachers are not using information yielded from the myriad of assessments to guide their instruction. We are not seeing the literate forest through the overassessed trees.

Although there is currently a raging debate about the relative merits of assessment methodology and execution, most teachers agree that some assessment mechanism is a necessary component of quality reading instruction. The current discussion evaluates numerous assessment programs and speaks to teachers contending with a spectrum of assessment methods. We are most concerned with helping teachers best use the assessment tools they respect and those they are required to administer.

How should teachers best use quality assessments? The answer to this question is deceptively simple: Teachers need to begin concentrating on how to use the information garnered through assessments to help students become better readers. Although this sounds like a simple solution, it presents a daunting task.

In the three sections of this book we aspire to help teachers face this often-elusive challenge. The first section of the book explores reading assessment and examines the role of assessment in exemplary teaching. The second section discusses how to improve reading instruction by effectively using assessment information to help children become strategic and fluent readers. The third section is set up in an easy-to-use format. Each lesson is divided into the following headings:

1. What do you hear and see?
2. Why does it matter?
3. What do you do?
4. What can the reader do independently and collaboratively?

When appropriate lessons include a fifth heading entitled What can family members/caregivers do?

What Do You Hear and See?

In the "What do you hear and see?" sections we describe what a classroom teacher might observe a student doing as she reads. Perhaps she is ignoring punctuation, maybe she reads a word for no apparent reason, or perhaps she reads fluently but lacks comprehension. This section contains many vignettes from our experiences and discusses diverse situations. The groupings of children vary and include whole group, small group, and individual encounters with children.

Why Does It Matter?

In the "Why does it matter?" sections we discuss the importance of the reader's current process as it is revealed through assessment. It is critical that we be informed about all aspects of the reader's construction of meaning and that we value the importance of child-centered instruction. To help children become more strategic readers, we need to understand what each miscue reveals.

What Do You Do?

The "What do you do?" sections contain tips, ideas, and suggestions intended to enable teachers to help students become better readers. We suggest specific dialogues and questions. These are intended to jump-start teachers' own thinking.

What Can the Reader Do Independently and Collaboratively?

In the "What can the reader do independently and collaboratively?" sections we suggest that students need to "test their strategic wings" after guided practice. We aim to help teachers impart skills and strategies for students to try on their own.

What Can Family Members and Caregivers Do?

Finally, in the "What can family members and caregivers do?" sections we provide "reproducibles" and ideas to share with family members and caregivers when appropriate. We believe that family members and caregivers truly want to help their children learn. They are invaluable partners in encouraging young readers.

PART I

What We Believe About Reading

We would like to begin with our list of nonnegotiables related to literacy instruction that reflect what we believe about how children learn to read and write across grade levels. Our list includes

- Basing instruction on authentic assessment
- Demonstrating reading, writing, and thinking aloud daily
- Utilizing shared and guided reading strategies often
- Using a workshop format to teach reading and writing
- Using minilessons and student-specific conferences to meet the needs of all students
- Having independent reading and writing daily
- Using quality children's literature for instruction

The practices we use to develop readers are closely related to what we believe to be best literacy practice. The assessments we use; the books, materials, and minilessons (a brief three- to five-minute lesson with a small group of children with like needs) we choose; the ways in which we listen to children read; and the questions we ask all reflect our deeply rooted beliefs about learning. These beliefs include the following:

- Knowledge is internally constructed.
- Social interaction or exchanging points of view with others is necessary for children to learn.
- Teachers, other adults, and peers can ask questions that help facilitate children's thinking.
- Listening and reading are processes that help humans gain information.

- Writing and speaking are processes that humans use to share their thinking with others.
- Motivation to learn must be intrinsic or can come from within rather than extrinsic or coming from the outside.
- Self-selection of reading texts and writing topics promotes increased learning.

What Is Reading?

Who in your class would you say is a good reader? Upon what information do you base your answer? These seemingly simple questions quickly become challenging to answer. Who you consider to be a good reader may not be a good reader in the eyes of the teacher across the hall. Teachers have varying views of the reading process. There are as many answers to the proposed question as there are readers. Let's take a closer look at several readers and discuss what each one reveals about your beliefs regarding reading.

Reader I   This third grade student can decode a list of sight words at the junior high level. She can read on or above grade-level text very fast and far exceeds the rate expected by the publishers of tests or mandated by the state department of education. However, she experiences much difficulty retelling what has been read. Thankfully, the student still feels confident about reading and refers to many high marks on comprehension and fluency tests.

Reader II   This fifth grade student is a very slow, deliberate reader who makes many miscues when reading. Most deviations from the text or miscues do not result in a meaning loss. The reader often ignores punctuation and often rereads after long phrases and sentences in an effort to construct meaning. During a retelling, the student can recount all the details of the text, which demonstrates strong comprehension.

Reader III   This first grade student cannot pronounce nonsense words (small groups of letters that aren't real words) on benchmark tests of a commercial program. The student does not excel at this exercise because she is trying to make each nonsense word into an authentic word. The student reads slowly and generates numerous miscues that are usually self-corrected. The retelling reflects ideas that are close to the author's meaning.

Reader IV   This sixth grade student simply stops reading whenever there is a multisyllabic word in the sentence. After much urging by the teacher, the student will go on and read until there is another long word in the text. The retellings have many misconceptions as a result of the missed multisyllabic words.

Which of these readers is more likely a student in your classroom? If you selected readers II and III as students from your classroom, you hold a psycholinguistic view of the reading process. If you chose readers I and IV, you hold a more behavioristic view of the reading process.

Psycholinguistic View

The psycholinguistic view of the reading process is the notion that the reading process is a four-legged stool. As Gollasch (1982) explains, readers use four cueing systems simultaneously as they read: graphophonics (features of letters), syntax (word order and relationship of words), semantics (meaning), and pragmatics (knowledge of how texts work). The brilliance of the psycholinguistic view is that whenever you read with a student or analyze your own reading process, every aspect of this view is verified as readers use the four cueing systems.

We hold a psycholinguistic view of the reading process. We believe that a reader must construct meaning from the print being read, or the process is simply decoding and relying on just one cueing system (graphophonic). Students also predict the words in the text that will come next based on their knowledge of written language. If the student has heard the genre read aloud many times, this knowledge will be used in predicting the next words and phrases. You often see this manifested with primary-age children who chime in on "Once upon a time . . ." as they hear the beginning of a fairy tale. Additionally, we observe how readers confirm or disconfirm what they are reading as they construct meaning about the text. If the reader can make sense of what has been read, confirmation of their prediction has occurred, but if the meaning doesn't make sense, the reader must reread to make sense of the text.

Because reading for meaning is paramount to us, oral fluency, which includes reading rate and expression, takes a back seat. We do *not* suggest that fluency is unimportant, but we have worked with many successful readers who were poor oral readers because they made many miscues. However, they completely understood every word they read.

We want our students to read age-appropriate text. Age-appropriate text is simply defined as a level of difficulty usually read by a particular age group. We are not concerned with whether a student is reading a text some educators might define as "frustrational" (more than five percent of words inaccurate) if the student is constructing meaning and is interested in the text. We don't use the terms *frustrational, instructional* (less than five percent of words inaccurate), and *independent* (all words correct), because we don't find the words helpful in describing the needs of students. We are only interested in whether a student constructs meaning.

Considering the reader's prior knowledge or life experiences is especially important to us because we know how necessary it is for the student to understand what has been read. All readers, from emergent to mature, must have some degree of prior knowledge of the text. If you are asked to read a passage about the genetics of fruit flies and you have no prior knowledge of the topic, it will be very challenging to construct meaning. Sometimes when we are reading with a student, we assume there is prior knowledge about a topic, but upon asking questions, we discover the problem is related to a lack of background information and not a lack of comprehension strategies.

The self-selection of real literature is critical because we want students to grapple with the content, be enthusiastic about reading, view reading as an interesting recreational activity, and to read for varied purposes. Because we love children's literature, we want our students to have favorite authors, illustrators, and genres. We want to instill in our children a passion for reading that will last them a lifetime.

Skills View

Teachers who hold a skills view of the reading process value an oral reader who seldom mispronounces an unknown word, always reads with expression, utters few miscues, and reads a certain number of words per minute. Some teachers associate good readers with good grades that appear on report cards. Other teachers may even view students who earn high scores on computerized tests like the STAR (STAR Reading, 2006) as automatically good readers.

A skills teacher holds a behaviorist view of learning and believes in an associationist notion that reading is simply connecting a particular oral sound with a letter of the alphabet. Comprehension is viewed as a phenomenon that happens only after the student can sound out all the words. Thankfully, we can't remember the name of the "expert" who contended the blue bird of comprehension would land on the child's shoulder after the sounding out of a word. We often speak of the notion that some educators teach as though comprehension is a fairy who finally dusts readers when they have mastered decoding.

Knowing if a student reads at an independent, frustrational, or instructional level is important to the skills-based teacher. Knowing the grade level of a particular text is also meaningful to those who come from a skills-based philosophy. Practicing skills with worksheets and games is a daily routine. Reading self-selected trade books or children's literature is an activity allowed only after assigned work has been completed.

The following table lists the major points of both a psycholinguistic and a skills view of reading:

Psycholinguistic View	Skills View
• Uses quality children's literature as basis of reading program	• Relies on commercial programs including decodable text

PSYCHOLINGUISTIC VIEW	SKILLS VIEW
• Embeds phonics instruction in authentic, daily reading and writing instruction	• Teaches phonics in isolation
• Focuses on students constructing meaning from text	• Focuses on sounding out words and speed
• Uses authentic reading and writing activities daily	• Uses worksheets and endless drills
• Uses assessment to guide instruction	• Assesses for reading grade level
• Demonstrates reading and writing frequently	• Demonstrates reading and writing infrequently
• Engages in read-alouds often	• Engages in read-alouds occasionally
• Teaches vocabulary within context	• Teaches vocabulary in isolation

What Is Effective Teaching of Reading?

Let us say that there are no perfect reading teachers, and the teachers we know whom we consider to be excellent would never make such a claim. The consummate professionals we know would tell you they are still "green and growing," continuing their learning so they can meet the many needs of the readers in their classrooms. However, there are some tenets we subscribe to about good teaching of reading, and we present them in the following paragraphs.

Psychological Environment

It is paramount in the teaching of reading to build a sense of community in your classroom where students feel comfortable and valued. If you haven't read *Life in a Crowded Place* by Ralph Peterson (1992), consider using it as a personal checklist to community building. All children must be respected for the unique individuals they are and for their choices of books and writing topics. The belief that everyone is a reader and a writer must permeate the classroom. An air of acceptance surrounds the miscues the reader makes, the invented spellings they write, and the unique contributions they make to the classroom.

Physical Environment

Creating a classroom that celebrates print is much easier to achieve than the building of an accepting psychological environment. It takes time to furnish a classroom library with many different genres, a variety of authors of books appropriate for your age group, books with illustrators that you and the children appreciate, poetry collections that make children laugh and cry, magazines, environmental print for young children, and rich nonfiction. Filling a classroom with excellent children's literature, and displaying it in a pleasing way, can take years. Do not expect the process of creating a pleasing physical environment to be a quick one. The three of us, with a combined total of more than 50 years in education, are still passionate collectors of children's literature.

Appreciation and Study of Children's Literature

We believe that to be effective teachers of reading we must have a vast knowledge and collection of children's literature. We began our lives and teaching careers with a love of children's literature. We each credit our mothers who instilled within each of us our love of books. As adults, Maryann was lucky enough to have Lyle Skov mentor her. Shelly and Clark have had Roberta Long, mentor and friend, guide them throughout their careers, turning them both into certifiable children's book-aholics. We strive daily to bring at least one new children's book into our lives, so we can personally enjoy them and share them with children. There are countless days we surpass that quota by *many* books!

An Understanding of the Relationship Between Reading and Writing

Young children learn to read and write simultaneously. We are students of the work of Emilia Ferrerio and know that literacy does indeed begin long before children are five. The seminal work of Ferrerio and Teberosky (1982) in *Literacy before Schooling* revealed how young children construct knowledge as they make sense of their environment, and how they begin to discern what is reading and how to invent spelling.

The cueing systems (graphophonics, syntax, semantics, pragmatics) are used each time young children use invented spelling to express ideas. We help our students read like writers and write like readers.

A Repertoire of Reading Strategies That Includes Daily Reading Aloud, Shared, Guided, and Independent Reading

New Zealand teachers remind us that a child needs to hear 1000 books before formal reading instruction begins. Although most educators favor reading aloud to young children, occasionally the need for continued reading aloud is overlooked. Much can be learned about written language from hearing quality children's literature read aloud. We can also teach a great deal about comprehension from modeling think-alouds and asking questions. Recommended texts about this topic are Mary Lee Hahn's book *Reconsidering Read-aloud* (2000) and Mem Fox's *Reading Magic* (2001).

Shared reading, a re-creation of lap reading done in the classroom, is a technique introduced by Don Holdaway (1979). It is a strategy for emergent readers that best supports children as they learn about print. Children learn a great deal about print as they read together with a teacher, enjoying the book over and over. During shared reading, teachers use an enlarged children's book or big book for an entire class to see, or they use a regular-size children's book with a small group of children or individual child. During the interaction, the teacher gives total support to all children, whether they are just beginning to construct knowledge about reading left to right or using word order and applying their knowledge of phonics. A recommended text to learn more about shared reading is Bobbi Fisher and Emily Medvic's book, *Perspectives on Shared Reading* (2000).

In the intermediate grades we use a shared read-aloud model during minilessons. There are some key differences between a shared read-aloud and a traditional read-aloud. During a shared read-aloud, children are actively engaged in applying or observing specific reading strategies and are considering important ideas and information. The format is interactive, yet somewhat structured in that the teacher has carefully planned the experience to meet the instructional needs of the readers. Although we are still advocates for traditional read-alouds that purely celebrate a love of language and books, we believe that authentic literature is the best teaching tool for students in all grades. Although shared reading in the primary grades focuses on word-solving strategies and book-handling skills, a shared read-aloud focuses on deep comprehension and reflection. Because the text in a shared read-aloud is not oversized, it is imperative that students gather together in close proximity to ensure that all readers can see the illustrations and feel connected to the book being shared.

When a child possesses one-to-one correspondence with the words of a shared reading text, guided reading follows. A small group of children who are on approximately the same text level and have similar needs meet with the teacher to read and learn together. The teacher offers support as the students learn and practice reading strategies. Irene Fountas and Gay Sue Pinnell have written extensively about guided reading. If you are a teacher of younger children, consider their book *Guided Reading: Good First Teaching for All Children* (1996). If you teach older children, look for their book *Guiding Readers and Writers (Grades 3–6)* (2001).

Independent reading occurs at different times for individual students. Some children reread the books used for guided reading and read predictable books until they have the strategies and confidence to attempt a piece of literature alone. There is no strategy that has the rewards of independent reading.

An author who writes about the value of independent reading is Richard Allington. Look for his books, including *What Really Matters for Struggling Readers: Designing Research-Based Programs* (2005).

Daily Reading and Writing Workshop

A large block of time should be designated during your day as a reading and writing workshop. This time should be sacred and protected from interruption. The workshops include time for read-aloud, shared, guided, and independent reading as well as process writing. Literacy centers that allow children independent practice can also be included during this time. Literature circles—small groups of children reading and discussing a piece of literature—are often held during reading and writing workshop time. The most common use of workshop time includes a whole group time at the beginning followed by time during which students read and write independently. At this time, the teacher works with children individually or in small groups. The workshop concludes with another whole group gathering during which sharing of reading and writing takes place. There are many excellent books that describe a workshop approach. Lucy Calkins' *The Art of Teaching Reading* (2001a) is an excellent source for learning more about reading workshops. Donald Graves' *A Fresh Look at Writing* (1994) is a good book about process writing that describes the elements of a writing workshop.

Authentic Assessment That Includes a Knowledge of Miscue Analysis

Good reading instruction must be preceded by quality assessment. When we receive our class list for the year, many questions race through our minds:

- How will I meet all their needs?
- Will they be as passionate about learning as I am?
- Will I be able to create a classroom community like last year's class? What will be the same about this group? What will be different?
- Who will our favorite authors/illustrators be?
- What will be their favorite genre?
- Which book should I read aloud first?

As the school year begins and as soon as we can steal the time from all our other beginning-of-the-year teacher duties, we anxiously assess the reading of each of our new students. For teachers who teach in middle and secondary schools, individual assessment often isn't possible because of the sheer numbers of students they have. Fortunately, most primary and intermediate teachers have self-contained classes with numbers that are manageable. We recommend beginning your assessments with students who seem to comprehend the least from what they are reading. Maryann calls this process of deciding who to assess first as *literacy triage*. At this time you are considering the group and looking for the most serious needs. You will work with those children first and continue until you have assessed each student.

There are several different instruments we use to assess oral reading. We like to include a retelling so we can understand the reader's comprehension abilities. We admit that we are partial to the reading miscue inventory (RMI) developed by Yetta Goodman, Dorothy Watson, and Carolyn Burke (2005), because it is based on a psycholinguistic view of the reading process and yields the most comprehensive look at a student's process of reading.

All miscues are analyzed under the lens of whether meaning is changed, if the miscue is similar graphically or audibly, and if the changed text still sounds like language. We recommend you learn to do an RMI procedure I, because this procedure requires you to analyze each miscue carefully. This assessment will add depth to your understanding of the reading process. Eventually you will use a simplified form of miscue analysis. After completing the analysis of a miscue in procedure I, you will automatically ask yourself: Was there a meaning change? Is the miscue syntactically acceptable? Is the miscue graphophonically similar? Does the miscue sound similar to the author's word? It is our view that if you rush and begin with the more simplified miscue analysis forms, you won't have a full understanding of the RMI. Only after you have deep understanding of RMI procedure I, can you move on to one of the several modifications of the RMI. One we like is Sandra Wilde's *Miscue Analysis Made Easy* (2000).

An assessment we use for young children is Marie Clay's running record. We recommend this instrument be used to determine when emerging readers are ready to move from shared to guided reading. The running record is effective for emergent readers because it informs the teacher about a reader's strategies. An explanation of running records can be found in Clay's book *An Observation Survey of Early Literary Achievement* (2002).

There are numerous differences between miscue analysis and a running record. Their purposes are different in that a running record seeks to determine whether a student has one-to-one correspondence. A miscue analysis is used to understand the reading process of the student. A running record is generally used with a younger child or a student just learning to read whereas a miscue analysis is generally used with a more established reader. A running record uses familiar text. The running record is often done with a passage of less than 100 words and includes no retelling. Miscue analysis uses unfamiliar text. The miscue analysis requires that a student read a passage of at least 250 words, and it includes a retelling. Running records are more easily administered and yield less comprehensive information. Miscue analysis is more labor intensive, but provides a great deal of information. Make sure you are using the correct assessment to provide the results you are looking for. After you have a miscue mind and can listen with a miscue ear, you never read with a child the same way again.

The qualitative reading inventory (QRI) developed by Leslie and Burke (2006) is an informal assessment that first uses word lists to determine which passages to choose for the reader. Although we give little value to a child's ability to call isolated words in a list, the results often reveal how the child was taught and what instruction you may need to provide. For example, if the child can decode words above age-appropriate text, it is possible that only word calling was valued in the instructional program.

The word lists are followed by short fiction and nonfiction passages. Some attributes of the RMI are present in the QRI, because miscues are marked, counted, and analyzed according to acceptability. There is an unaided retelling section followed by a series of explicit and implicit comprehension questions.

There are many informal reading inventories (IRIs) that span more than forty years of reading instruction. Some of them analyze reading miscues, but many still count all miscues as errors with no qualitative examination. Another criticism of many IRIs is the lack of an unaided and aided retelling.

Good assessment information isn't just gathered during the administration of an assessment tool. Through careful observation you can learn much about a reader. A few of the opportunities you have to observe students are while listening to the child read aloud, while discussing meanings constructed in literature circles, while discussing the class read-aloud, while observing their book selections, and while listening to how students respond to literature during conferences. All this important information is gathered in many ways and should be recorded in some form, such as on sticky notes, index cards, and computer labels.

In recent years, many schools have purchased computer software that purports to assess reading abilities. It has been our observation that all these quick assessments have little or no value as reading assessments. Often, there is no correlation between a student's score on such a computer test and the student's actual ability to read.

Silent reading tests have been used in classrooms for many years and are still used today. These tests serve the purpose of determining whether independent readers are comprehending a text; however, they are limited because they do not provide insight into which strategies a reader is/is not using.

A problem with some assessments is that the results leave you with only a subjective grade level or "reading zone." Other assessments, such as the *Dominie Reading and Writing Assessment Portfolio* (2004) and the *Writing, Reading Assessment Profile (W.R.A.P),* tell you more. These assessments correlate with Pinnell and Fountas' guided reading levels (1996; 2001), and help both teacher and student identify appropriate texts for both guided and independent reading. When using the RMI and QRI you learn which cueing systems the reader is using, which is valuable information. However, teachers still struggle with text selection.

Summary

Assessment is just one of the many important aspects of our job as teachers. Knowing how to assess is an area that we continue to improve as long as we teach. Each of us has our own system that we change over time. In the next section of this book we look more fully at some of the different assessments that we find helpful as we teach reading.

II

What We Believe About Reading Assessment

There is always an element of assessment taking place whenever we are teaching, and this is especially true during literacy instruction. We are always assessing! When we are conducting a small group discussion, a minilesson, an individual conference, or observing students reading and writing, we are making mental notes about the student's process. Therefore, assessment is cyclical because we are always learning more about the reader or writer.

In this section we discuss the different types of assessment we find helpful in our teaching of reading. There is no one instrument that informs you about everything you need to know about a reader and writer. We make recommendations about what we find helpful and expedient, because a lack of time is every teacher's greatest challenge to overcome. In a perfect world we would have a small number of students with a 108-hour day so we could accomplish everything we want to do. Because we have little control over student numbers, and our days only contain 24 hours, we must settle for doing our best with the time we are given.

The first step in reading instruction must be assessment so we can plan effective instruction. For younger children, the question is: Where is the student in the process of becoming a reader and writer? For most older children and adolescents, the question is: What aspects of the reading or writing process are in need of enhancement?

We are not going to suggest that you have three-ring binders full of completed tests and filing cabinets bursting with progress monitoring sheets, all of which you consider only briefly. Some of your most valuable assessments may be notes on scraps of paper and mental notes that you make along the way.

How Often Should You Use a Commercial Assessment?

Although you are always assessing, the most important time to use commercial assessments is at the beginning of your teaching of the student, which is most often at the beginning of the school year. You can't assess all the students immediately with a formal assessment, so remember to begin by choosing the students who seem the most mysterious to you.

Younger students who are emerging as readers will need more frequent assessment than older students who are using cueing systems and reading age-appropriate text or above. Some kindergarten and first grade teachers do running records as often as every two weeks. They do them quickly during the literacy block. Assessment at the end of the year allows you to reflect, as you study your students' progress.

What About Standardized Test Scores?

As we suggested, at each level of schooling, different assessments are appropriate. We are not fans of high-stakes testing, so what we recommend isn't norm referenced. We will, however, suggest that if standardized scores are available, you review the reading comprehension scores to determine which students need to be assessed first. A sixth grader who has scored consistently above the 50th percentile for several years will probably not be your first priority for an individualized test. If you teach in a school in which most of the students are above the 75th percentile, then a student at the 50th percentile on reading comprehension may be a candidate for individual assessment.

What Is Most Important When We Assess Reading?

Among the three of us, we assess the reading strategies of hundreds of students each year. Each summer, during a reading program for students experiencing reading difficulties, Maryann assesses a couple hundred struggling readers. She doesn't have the luxury of a lot of time in which to do it. Teachers are waiting for her results and her recommendations about what strategies will support student growth. Speed is important, because the program is only six weeks long. There is no time to waste. Shelly works in a large elementary school. She assesses and helps teachers make instructional decisions about countless readers. Clark, in his second grade classroom, works closely with a group of students and administers both his own assessments as well as others mandated by district, state, and federal authorities. We share our experience with you because we want you to know that we have spent a lot of time either assessing or considering assessments. It is important for us to note that even with our extensive experience, there are some students who we consider mysterious, because we are unable to identify their strengths easily. Sometimes we are left unsure about what to recommend. When this happens, we consult colleagues for their opinions and advice.

Although we are each looking at assessment from our different roles, we agree on the following statements:

- Listening to a student read aloud unfamiliar text is valuable and necessary.
- Conducting an unaided and aided retelling is important.
- Asking a child to spell specific words reveals much about phonemic awareness and phonics development.
- Asking the child to pronounce sight words (real words, not nonsense words) is only helpful if you need guidance in the selection of the level of real text, and can reveal much about how the child was taught to read.
- Conducting a reading interview can improve your understanding of a student's notions about the reading process.
- The power of observing students or "kidwatching" can't be underestimated.

What Assessment Should You Use?

This question has many answers that depend on whether the student is emergent and the level of text the student can read. Also, many teachers must use mandated assessments even if they don't view them as valuable. We make recommendations about the ones we use, but there are certainly good assessments of which we are not informed.

What Do You Need to Know About the Student's Reading?

The following are attributes we find invaluable about a reader and the assessments we use to find the information.

- *Cueing systems*—Which ones do the students use (graphophonic, syntactic, semantic, and pragmatic)?
- *Notions about the reading process*—What are the reader's ideas about what reading and writing instruction are?
- *Reading interests*—What are the genre and topics of books that the student self-selects?
- *Attitudes toward reading*—Does the student view reading as a pleasurable activity and choose independent reading when given options?
- *Appropriate (approximate) level of text*—What is the approximate level of text that the student can read with support for guided reading?
- *Fluency*—Is rate and/or expression interfering with comprehension?

- *Vocabulary size*—Does the student possess a large pool of commonly used words?
- *Retelling abilities*—Can the student retell what has been read?
- *General knowledge*—Is the student's background of information sufficient to understand texts recommended for the age group?

READING ASSESSMENT INFORMATION AND SOURCES

Information	Assessment
Graphophonic cueing	• Clay letter identification including sound and word tasks • Kamii and Manning spelling word list • Student writing analysis • RMI • Running record analysis • Observation of reading miscues
Syntactic cueing	• RMI • Observation of reading miscues • Student writing analysis
Semantic cueing	• RMI, including unaided and aided retellings • Observation of reading miscues • Prior knowledge questions • Observation of contributions during text discussions
Pragmatic cueing	• Observation of predictions in unfamiliar text
Notions about reading	• Burke reading interview for younger and older readers (Goodman et al. 2005)
Reading interests	• Observing choices • Listening for enthusiasm in choices • Recording favorite genres and topics of books in self-selection book records
Appropriate (approximate) level of text	• Guided reading text, guided reading records • Independent reading text, self-selection book records • QRI

(continues)

READING ASSESSMENT INFORMATION AND SOURCES (CONTINUED)	
Information	**Assessment**
Fluency	• Listening to students read different types of texts for rate and expression
Vocabulary size	• Listening to students' oral language

Retelling abilities	• For unaided and aided retellings
	  o Use the RMI
	  o Listen during discussions of literature

General knowledge	• Listening to the amount of background information during discussions

Observing (Kidwatching)

Kidwatching is of utmost importance because standardized and informal tests cannot replace your professional judgment. Each day we teach, we become better at kidwatching. There is much we can learn each minute we are with our students. Yetta Goodman, the educator who coined the term *kidwatching*, has written extensively on the topic. Excellent books on the topic are Sandra Wilde's (1996) edited book, *Notes from a Kidwatcher: Selected Writings of Yetta M. Goodman,* and Gretchen Owocki and Goodman's book (2002), *Kidwatching: Documenting Children's Literacy Development.*

From Goodman we have learned there is no aspect of language, either oral or written, that we can't observe and learn from the student. She says, "We can collaborate with children, find out what they are doing and why, and celebrate their intellectual abilities as they experiment with written language" (Goodman, Bird, and Goodman 1991, 356). We want to trust our kidwatching and continue to increase our abilities with each student with whom we are fortunate enough to interact.

Reading Miscue Inventory

The RMI developed by Goodman, Watson, and Burke (2005) has been invaluable to us in our understanding of the reading process and of individual student's reading. We found that learning about the miscue analysis inventory was a turning point in our development as teachers of reading. We recommend that you learn how to do an RMI procedure I, the most complete version that analyzes all aspects of the reading process, even if you are mandated to use another assessment. You may ask why; the reason is simple. After we learned how to do an RMI, we didn't view the reading process in the same way. We began valuing all miscues, even if meaning was lost; therefore, the RMI was definitely a milestone in our professional lives. We present a very simplified explanation of the process and encourage you to read the original publication.

A miscue is any oral reading deviation from what is written in the text. A miscue can be a word or punctuation change. You are looking for miscues that change meaning and those that don't change meaning. You are also analyzing the miscues to determine whether they have similar letters (graphically similar), whether they sound like language (syntactically correct), and whether they make sense (semantically correct).

Types of Miscues

Substitutions   With substitutions, one word is substituted for another. Example: The author's word is *banana* and the reader says *fruit*. In some instances there would be no meaning loss. For example, if the sentence was, "*There was a banana in the salad*," substituting *fruit* would not, in most cases, really change the meaning. Although *fruit* for *banana* isn't graphically similar, it is both syntactically and semantically correct. The substituted word is written over the original word.

Corrections   With corrections, the reader says one word and then realizes that her prediction was incorrect. The word is then changed to the correct word. For instance, the reader says, "The horse, house was full of insects." The correction doesn't change meaning and indicates that the reader is monitoring meaning because the sentence doesn't make sense if the word is *horse*.

Horse for *house* is graphically similar, is syntactically correct, but is not semantically correct because the word *horse* didn't make sense. The reader corrected the miscue so there was no loss in meaning. The correction is marked with a circled SC to denote self-correction.

Repetitions   With repetitions, the word or phrase is repeated once or twice while the reader is predicting what comes next in the sentence. Example: The reader says, "The house is, The house is" before completing the sentence with "falling down." Repeating the three words does not change the meaning. Repeated words are underlined each time they are repeated.

Reversals   With reversals, a word is said before another word that comes first in the sentence. For example the text says, The baby is crying again. And the reader says, The baby is again crying. There is no change in meaning. Reversals are marked with a sideways letter "s."

Omissions   With omissions, a word is omitted during the reading. For example, the text says, "The old man walked down the road." The reader says, "The man walked down the road." In many stories, the omission of "old" would not really affect meaning. Omitted words are circled.

Insertions   With insertions a word is added to a sentence. For instance, the text says, "We will go to the concert on Friday." The reader says, "We will go out to the concert on Friday." This insertion of "out" does not change meaning and sounds like the reader's home-rooted language. Inserted words are marked with a caret.

Other, less frequent types of miscues in the RMI include misarticulations, dialect, split syllables, pauses, and intonation shifts. Only the most common miscues are described here. Please refer to the RMI for a complete listing.

There are numerous marking systems and no one system is better than another. We prefer the marking used in the RMI. The important thing is that you be consistent so you can interpret what the reader has said when you refer to the transcript at a later time. For example, if everyone circles omitted words there is little room for misinterpretation. It is also advantageous for teachers in the same school to be somewhat consistent in their markings from grade level to grade level, so assessments can be understood as students and assessments travel from one teacher to the next.

Parts of a Miscue Analysis

The description here is brief and the reader will want to consult the *Reading Miscue Inventory* (Goodman et al. 2005) for more details.

Assessment Preparation   You choose an unfamiliar text that you believe will cause the student to make miscues. After the student is comfortable, tell her that she will read the text and that she should pretend that you are not there if she comes to a word she doesn't know. Also, tell her that you will be asking her to tell you about the text after the reading. You will be tape-recording the oral reading and the retellings so you will want to check that your tape recorder is set loud enough so you can hear the recording when you replay it.

Oral Reading   Give the reader an opportunity to sample the text. The reader reads the text without your assistance. If the student produces none or only a few miscues, you will need to select a more difficult text. If the student makes so many miscues that you believe it is not possible for meaning to be constructed, you should select a less difficult text.

When selecting texts, choose a complete text and not a book chapter. There should be a minimum of 250 words, and the authors of the procedure recommend a 500-word text.

Unaided Retelling   After the reading of the text, ask the student to tell you everything she remembers from the text while you make notes.

Aided Retelling   During this part of the procedure you ask questions based on the unaided retelling information. You ask questions about plot and theme statements, characters, inferences, and misconceptions the reader may have revealed.

Analysis of the Oral Reading   The miscues are charted in procedure I to determine their graphophonic, syntactic, and semantic acceptability, as well as sound and graphic similarity and grammatical relationship. The total number of words and number of miscues are calculated to determine the percentage of miscues. The emphasis is, however, on the strengths the reader brought to the text rather than on the weaknesses.

Analysis of the Retellings   This aspect of the inventory is especially important because students can make meaning-loss miscues and still construct the author's meaning. The focus on this part is only about whether the student comprehended the author's meaning of the text.

There are several different miscue analysis inventory forms. After you become proficient with procedure I, there is no reason why you can't experiment with other forms. Sandra Wilde has alternative forms in her book, *Miscue Analysis Made Easy: Building on Student Strengths* (2000).

Running Records   Developed by Marie Clay from New Zealand, this system is one that many teachers find useful for emergent readers. Although Clay has proposed the procedure for more mature readers, we only use it for emergent readers who can't read a 250-word text. Here are some of the differences that we believe exist between the two procedures.

RUNNING RECORDS	MISCUE ANALYSIS
The purpose is to determine whether a child has one-to-one correspondence.	The purpose is to determine processes used when reading.
Familiar text is used.	Unfamiliar text is used.
Any length of text can be used.	Text should be a minimum of 250 words.
No retelling is used.	Unaided and aided retelling is used.

Qualitative Reading Inventory

A much shorter form of assessment is the QRI, but it doesn't yield the information of the RMI. The fiction and nonfiction texts are much shorter than a real RMI, but this inventory does embody some of the important concepts of miscue analysis.

A sight word test is used for placement of the reader in the different levels of text. When we use the sight word list, we find that we often learn about how the student was previously instructed in reading. We test students who say every sight word quickly and who know a large percentage of words from lists that are well above what is age appropriate. Unfortunately, the sight word whiz kids are unable to retell text at a similar level. Often the level at which they are able to comprehend what they have read is several levels below what the sight word results would lead you to believe. We conclude from listening to the child read that the sole emphasis of their previous reading instruction was on calling words because of their inability to comprehend the text. An unaided retelling is also included. Miscues are also analyzed to determine which ones change meaning.

Modifying Informal Reading Inventories

Teachers are often required to use inventories that count errors instead of miscues, and are more concerned with accuracy and rate rather than with comprehension. We find that we can often modify these inventories by adding a retelling and analyzing the miscues to determine what percentage changed the meaning.

Assessing Graphophonic Knowledge

Although you can learn much about phonics from invented spelling, we recommend using the Marie Clay letter identification task in her book, *An Observation Survey of Early Literacy Achievement* (2002). After you ask a child to say the letter names, follow the directions and ask the child to say the sounds of the letters. After sounds, ask the child to say a word that begins with the sound of the letter. To assess phonics information such as blends, digraphs, and diphthongs, ask the child to spell two or three words that contain the pattern.

We assess many students who have conflicting views about how to use the phonics knowledge they possess. Many students, when asked to write the words we use for spelling assessment (ocean, cement, vacation, punishment, motion, tomato, and karate), will reflect their confusion by adding *e*'s to all words and adding *e* and *y* when they write an *i*. They also ask us questions like, "How many vowels does this word have?" Or they make statements like, "I can't remember the rule for that one."

We find that, in sharp contrast to our recommendations, school psychologists and private psychometrists usually recommend to teachers and parents that the child should receive more phonics instruction. Many times the recommendations are based on the fact that the student may have only been tested on phonics and phonemic awareness knowledge. Seldom do we meet a student who is older than seven years old who doesn't know most sound–letter correspondences.

Spelling Assessment

Why do we believe that spelling is an important assessment related to the reading process? Spelling assessment tells us about the child's phonemic awareness and also about his phonographic knowledge.

Elementary students range in spelling from drawing pictures to using conventional spelling. You can assess phonemic awareness through progress in invented spelling, and much can also be learned about phonetic knowledge by observing a child's writing.

You can quickly assess a student's spelling ability by asking her to spell the following words individually: *ocean, cement, vacation, punishment, motion, tomato,* and *karate.* These are not just randomly selected words, but ones that we have been using in research studies. *Ocean, vacation,* and *motion* have a pattern. *Punishment* and *cement* have another pattern. Careful attention to how the student spells each word pattern does or does not reveal a logical system. *Tomato* and *karate* are especially effective in tapping both phonemic awareness abilities and graphophonic knowledge.

After the student has written the words, you can qualitatively analyze the spelling. Remember, you are not looking for correct spelling, but rather for the logic the student is using and the level of development. Because spelling is social knowledge, it is necessary for the child to have been in an environment in which there was information about print.

Because we are students of the work of Emilia Ferreiro, and Maryann has done a lot of research with Constance Kamii replicating Ferreiro's research in English, you will find a similarity between Ferreiro's levels and the ones we are sharing. The amount of literacy episodes (hearing literature read aloud and observing adults read and write) in a child's preschool years is usually reflected in his spelling level.

Levels of Spelling

Pictures   The child draws a picture when the spelling of a word is requested. If a kindergarten child draws a picture of a tomato when asked to spell "tomato," the child may have a written language delay.

Level I   The child uses letter strings in which there are often undifferentiated letter shapes strung across a piece of paper. (See Figure 1.1.)

Level II   The child uses a minimum and maximum number of letters (usually varies from three to seven letters) to represent words. There is no letter–sound correspondence at this level. (See Figure 1.2.)

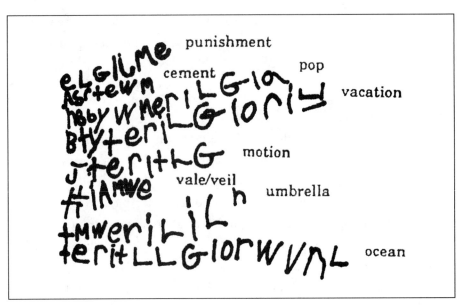

FIGURE 1.1 Level I

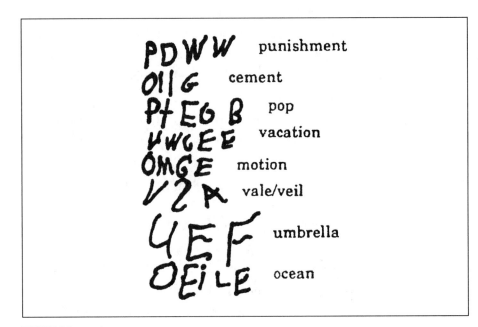

FIGURE 1.2 Level II

Level III   This is the consonantal level because the child only uses consonants and letter name words. This is the level where you can read with difficulty the invented spelling. (See Figure 1.3.)

Level IV   The child begins to add short vowels to the words that can now be read with little difficulty. (See Figure 1.4.)

Level V   This level is conventional spelling when most words are spelled correctly.

Pnmt
punishment
Cmnt
cement
PP
pop
VKn
vacation
mon
motion
VL
vale/veil
mBKL
umbrella
oen
ocean

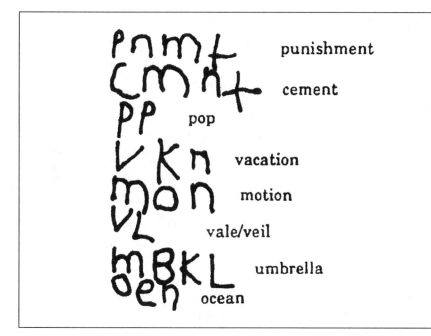

FIGURE 1.3 Level III

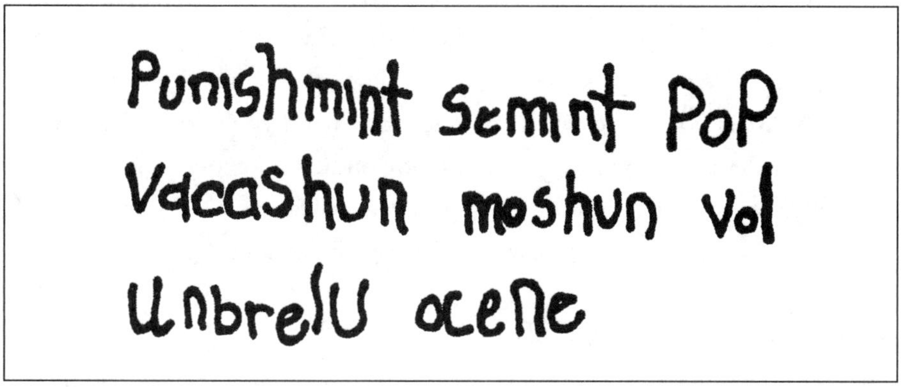

Punishmint Semnt PoP
Vacashun moshun Vol
Unbrelu ocene

FIGURE 1.4 Level IV

For more information about the spelling levels refer to Kamii, Long, Manning, and Manning's (1990) article "Spelling in Kindergarten: A Constructivist Analysis Comparing Spanish-Speaking and English-Speaking Children."

Phonemic Awareness

Although this book is about refining readers, there are those who believe that lack of phonemic awareness is a serious reading problem. We know that children who can read possess phonemic awareness, but we have had difficulty finding many children beyond six years old, readers and nonreaders, who do not possess this cognitive skill.

You can very easily assess phonemic awareness by asking the child to say some words and then analyze their responses. Demonstrate how to say a word in phonemes. (We say little bites because many children understand that concept.) First ask the child to say some two-syllable words in phonemes such as *pony*, *tepee*, and *sofa*.

Level I   No differentiation in the phonemes; the child says "pony."

Level II   The child separates the word at the syllables; the child says "po–ny."

Level III   The child separates one of the syllables into phonemes but leaves one syllable whole; the child says "p-o-ny" or "po-n-y."

Level IV   The child separates both syllables into phonemes; the child says, "p-o-n-e-y."

For more information refer to Kamii and Manning's (2002) article, "Phonemic Awareness and Beginning Reading and Writing."

Notions About the Reading Process

One of the easiest and most effective ways to find out what a student is thinking about the reading process is to use the Burke Reading Interview. Carolyn Burke has included ten questions in the interview such as the following: What is reading? What do you do when you come to a word you don't know? Who is a good reader that you know? How would you help someone who was having trouble reading? The Burke Reading Interview and sample responses can be found in the book *Reading Miscue Inventory* (Goodman et al. 2005).

Reading Interests

Once, Maryann heard Jerry Harste say that the competency test for a teacher should be whether she can name five topics that each of her students are interested in and want to learn about. The more we think about that statement the more we agree that knowing about the interests of our students is vitally important. How do we find out about interests? We know that some of our students will spout out everything they want to learn about, whereas there are others who are reticent to share.

We recommend that you have a notebook or a pack of note cards that you can use to jot down interests quickly. They don't need to be alphabetized on the sheet or card. You just need to be able to find them when you need them to recommend a book or writing topic. Students share what they like throughout the day, and sometimes it is at lunch or on the playground that we learn the most. Sometimes you notice an interest during the discussion of a read-aloud, or during social interactions in social studies or science.

Writing Ability

You will never meet a writer who isn't a reader, but the opposite isn't always true. Although we are not addressing writing directly, we do find that studying a student's writing can reveal information that is useful in reading. Carl Anderson's book *Assessing Writers* (2005) offers a comprehensive approach to looking at students' writing and can be very helpful as you consider assessment. We mentioned the need to keep a record of interests because you can make recommendations if a student experiences a block and can't think of anything to write about during writers' workshop.

Students Assessing Themselves— Retrospective Miscue

Yetta Goodman, Ann Marek (1996), and others have written extensively about retrospective miscue, a procedure for students to analyze their own miscues while improving their reading process. Teachers using retrospective miscue analysis first discuss the most common miscues (substitutions, omissions, repetitions) and then demonstrate how the students can mark miscues on an enlarged copy of the text.

The students work in pairs or triads and tape-record each other reading aloud. After the oral reading they compare the recording with the text and mark miscues without using a formal system.

After the students have marked their transcript, the teacher meets with them to examine miscues. Just as we look at each miscue to determine whether there is a meaning loss or change, we ask our students if the miscue changed the meaning, if it sounded like oral language, if it made sense, if the word looked like the author's word, and why they think they made the miscue. The longer they help each other analyze their own reading process, the more they grow in their confidence as readers. A book that contains practical applications of retrospective miscue is Rita Moore and Carol Gilles' book *Reading Conversations: Retrospective Miscue Analysis for Struggling Readers 4–12* (2005).

Summary

In this short review we have shared our favorite assessments. They are compatible with our philosophy of language learning and give us the information that we feel is necessary for us to plan meaningful instruction to support the development of our readers. In the next part, we share the instructional strategies we use in our teaching.

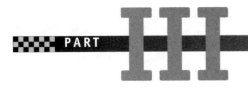

PART III

Lessons to Refine Readers

This section of the book highlights the lessons we have used to refine the readers in our classrooms as well as countless other classrooms belonging to our colleagues. Please keep the following points in mind as you use the lessons in your classroom:

- Each lesson is appropriate for all age groups.
- Each lesson can be made more or less difficult simply by changing the children's literature.
- Each reproducible page can be used in many different ways to suit your needs. You can use these pages with one student, a small group of students, or a whole group of students.
- Each reproducible page can easily be made into a classroom chart or used in a student's literature log.
- Each of the authors and illustrators chosen is one of our favorites. Make sure to incorporate your favorite authors and illustrators as well.

Acronyms

What do you hear or see?

While discussing a newspaper article with a student about space exploration, you observe that the student refers to NASA (the National Aeronautics and Space Administration) as N-A-S-A. When you attempt to model the correct usage of this acronym, the student gives you a look that makes it clear that NASA is not in this child's spoken vocabulary. You begin to wonder how many of your students know how to read acronyms.

Why does it matter?

Acronyms are everywhere. Between two and three million acronyms have been recorded, and online services can define almost all of them in seconds. This staggering number almost guarantees that students will encounter them frequently throughout their lives. Therefore, it is vital that we explore acronyms with children. Although it would be absurd to try to teach a set of specific acronyms, there are strategies for reading them effectively.

What do you do?

Teach your students about acronyms. When they are used in a text, they are often followed by *definitional context clues* that will register with the prior knowledge of the students. It is important to show children that acronyms are written in all capital letters. Sometimes periods separate the letters and sometimes they do not. Some acronyms are abbreviations that are read letter by letter. More accurately called *initialisms* (FBI, USA, USDA, and MIA), they are usually considered acronyms. True acronyms are abbreviations that are pronounced as words (FEMA, NATO, NASA). Although this may be too much information for many students, it will help explain why some acronyms are read as words and others are not. In simpler terms, when an acronym can be read easily as a word, it is.

We recommend you share examples of both types of acronyms with your students. In our experience, acronyms appear regularly in periodicals such as your local newspaper, *National Geographic Explorer*, and *Time for Kids*. They are also a part of fiction. In Jerry Spinelli's *Loser* (2002, 75), a frightening acronym is brought to light:

> "His brother went away to fight in the Vietnam War and was MIA and never came back."
>> Donald senses a sadness somewhere in the distance. "What's MIA?"
>> "Missing in action. It means they're pretty sure he was killed but they can't find his body."

In Gennifer Choldenko's *Al Capone Does My Shirts* (2004), acronyms and initialisms like UCLA, aka, and IOU are found throughout.

A discussion about acronyms will likely spark an interest in them. We suggest that you post a list of acronyms and their definitions in your classroom. Each time an acronym is encountered and discussed, the student who discovered it can add it to the list.

What can the reader do independently and collaboratively?

- Ask readers to be on the lookout for acronyms during independent reading. When a new acronym is found, ask the student to jot down both the acronym and its definition. If the acronym is not defined in the text, encourage the student to look for the definition using an online dictionary.
- Encourage students to use acronyms when they speak and write to show their understanding of them.

Create a learning center in which students match common acronyms to their definitions.

Dear family members and caregivers,

We have been talking about acronyms we encounter in both books and our daily lives. As adults, we use acronyms when we speak and when we write. We were amazed to learn that between two and three million acronyms have been documented across the world.

Some acronyms like NASA and IOU have been familiar to us. Others, such as aka and USDA have been a bit more challenging. You can help us become better readers by helping us expand our understanding of acronyms.

- Share acronyms that you use in your daily lives with your reader. They can, in turn, share them with us. We will add new acronyms to our classroom collection.

- Be on the lookout for acronyms in the environment. From cereal boxes and produce labels to billboards and store fronts, acronyms are everywhere.

- Remind your reader to notice acronyms in independent reading at home. If you know the definition of the acronym, share it. Encourage him or her to write down the acronym and its meaning so it can be shared with the class.

Thank you for helping us grow as readers.

Author's Purpose

What do you hear or see?

While generating questions about the book *Cecil's Story* by George Ella Lyon (1991) with a group of fourth grade students, a girl asks, "Why would she write this story?" This book of few words and detailed illustrations had already kept us riveted for almost an hour. Shelly and the students had discussed the text and illustration. They made deep connections between the text and the past. And yet the wrinkled nose on this child's face let Shelly know that the student was sincerely concerned. Thinking the student was disappointed with the book, she asked her to elaborate on her question. It became evident that the student had been moved by the story, but wanted to know why the author would write about what we inferred to be the US Civil War. "That was so long ago," she said. What was the author's purpose? Aren't there wars going on in the world today?

Why does it matter?

Authors write for a reason. Perhaps you are like us and you remember completing worksheets in school in which you read a short piece of text and then decided if the author's purpose was to inform the reader, entertain the reader, or persuade the reader. We were never allowed to consider that authors might write for a combination of these purposes or, perhaps more revolutionary, none of them at all. Perhaps you are a teacher who has presented similar worksheets to your students. We would ask you to reconsider and think about the reasons why authors truly write.

Although we have never had the pleasure of asking Lyon about her purpose for writing *Cecil's Story*, we seriously doubt that she would tell us it was to inform children about the Civil War, or to entertain them with a story about war, or to persuade them never to fight in a war. Instead, a group of fourth grade students concluded that she probably wrote this story to show us how children feel when their parents leave for a long time, be it going to work or going to war. They were also intrigued by the dedication page in which the author mentions her great-great grandparents by name. We were left to wonder if there were elements of biography in the story. The kids never really answered the "why" question, but they engaged in a deep discussion about the possibilities.

What do you do?

Discuss the author's purpose with your students, and do not restrict them. Are all picture books intended only to entertain? Who is to say that a nonfiction text couldn't be informative, entertaining, and persuasive at the same time?

Consider the book *Encounter* by Jane Yolen (1992a). This book explores Columbus's arrival in the New World from the perspective of the native Taino people of San Salvador. This picture book captivates children, so we guess you could call it entertaining, but to say that Yolen was simply trying to inform children about what happened to these people isn't likely. We believe she was trying to help us *feel* what the Taino felt. She was trying to help us challenge information we already thought we knew by presenting a side of the story that most children have never heard.

Another book that helps children discuss possible purposes for writing is *A Boy Called Slow* by Joseph Bruchac (1994). This picture book biography of Sitting Bull is definitely informative and entertaining, but it also teaches us a valuable lesson about judging people prematurely. In our experience children identify with Sitting Bull and often infer that Bruchac's purpose for writing this book was to show them that they, too, can overcome obstacles and accomplish great things.

Even truly entertaining books like *Wolf!* by Becky Bloom (1999) offer us more than a laugh when we let children do the thinking and the talking about the author's purpose. This book, popular with our youngest readers, tells the story of a wolf who sees the other animals reading and wants to learn to read himself. Yes, the author wants to make us laugh, which we gladly do. But the children we have discussed this text with also think the author is trying to *encourage* kids. Learning to read is hard work for many, and this author conveys the message that with support and practice, even the wolf learned to read.

What can the reader do independently and collaboratively?	• Write their ideas about the author's purpose in their journals. Do not limit the children with specific labels and phrases. They will amaze you with their insight.
	• Discuss the author's purpose with a small group in a center or during a book study. This collaborative setting allows for an exchange of ideas that will help children learn to consider perspectives other than their own. Our prior experiences flavor how we infer an author's purpose.

Dear family members and caregivers,

We have been talking about the reasons why authors write. Perhaps you are like me and you remember talking about the author's purpose when you were young. I recall being told that authors write for one of three reasons: to inform, to entertain, or to persuade. We now understand that authors write for *many* reasons, which may or may not include those we were taught. We have discussed how some authors write to encourage us to follow our dreams and others write to help us experience places we have never visited. Writers write for many reasons. You can help us better understand an author's purpose by

- Talking to your reader about what he or she is reading independently, both at home and at school. Discuss possible reasons the author wrote the book.

- Share your newspaper with your child. Choose an appropriate article of interest and read it together. Talk about the purpose of the article. Are all newspaper articles purely informative? Then read an appropriate editorial together. How are the purposes for the articles different?

- Discuss the purpose for the text on billboards, road signs, and/or store fronts as you move about your daily lives.

- Remind your reader that writers have many purposes in mind when they create books and articles for us.

Thank you for helping us grow as readers.

Appropriate Book Selection

What do you hear or see?

Through observations made during reading workshop and conferences held with a reader, you notice he is more often than not choosing books that are too difficult for him to read. These poor book selections pave the way for a myriad of misunderstandings and great frustration.

Why does it matter?

A couple of years ago, Shelly and Clark were conducting a professional development workshop for a group of elementary school teachers. The event was large enough to be held in the local high school. We were amazed at the condition of the building and the lack of materials we found in the classroom we were given to present in. Counting our blessings and unpacking our wares, we noticed a small hand-lettered sign in the otherwise bleak, desolate room. The sign simply read: THE CHILD WHO IS NOT READING HAS NOT FOUND THE RIGHT BOOK. That moment struck a chord within each of us and has stayed in our memories ever since. It is imperative that readers of any age read books they can comprehend. As classroom teachers, we all realize the fact that the more you read, the better reader you become. Children need our guidance in making appropriate choices of books to read. Even though your classroom may be a place of great student autonomy, don't hesitate to guide them in the direction of appropriate book selection.

What do you do?

Book selection strategies abound in professional literature, yet it seems, based on our visits to many classrooms, and as we stated earlier, that children are more often than not reading books that are simply too difficult. Readers need to be empowered to make the best choices in reading material. Some strategies for appropriate book selection we are using or have found to be helpful include

- Creating a classroom community in which all levels of reading are celebrated. Readers in a caring classroom community are never shunned by their peers based upon their reading choices.
- Either individually, in a small group, or as a class minilesson, explaining that just because a particular book is too difficult for today doesn't necessarily mean it will too difficult in the future. By not reading the book today, you are not saying you will never be able to read it.
- Offering the reader an alternate choice similar to the book they desire to read. The Harry Potter phenomenon has trickled down to second grade-age children who are just sure they can read one of J. K. Rowling's thick volumes. Clark has observed firsthand the pride his young charges take in being seen with such a large

book and the pride-filled remarks parents make when they say their child is reading a Harry Potter book. It is the rare second grader who can read and comprehend this challenging reading material. Often, the situation can be defused by simply offering a more appropriate choice. Young Harry Potter fans nearly always fall for Tony Abbott's *Secrets of Droon* (2002) series. A collection of dozens of books, they have the same magical quality found in the highly coveted Potter books, but are written in a voice that's more readily understood by a younger reader.

One particular book selection strategy we like and have used with success with children of all ages comes from an article entitled, "I Need a Good Book . . . FAST!" (Sharp 1992). The strategy offers children 12 questions to consider as they select an appropriate book. The aspects of the book the questions discuss spells out the acronym CAN IT BE FOR ME (which is included at the end of this lesson)? Each of the aspects can easily be taught in a minilesson.

What can the reader do independently and collaboratively?	The readers in your classroom will begin to internalize the strategies you have offered regarding book selection. Clark saw this happen firsthand about 12 weeks into the school year. Jordan, a struggling reader who so wanted to read chapter books, had a Post-It note and magic marker beside her as she began a new book. Clark immediately knew the choice was too difficult, but decided to observe what she would do next. On the small Post-It note, she repeatedly wrote two simple words: yes and no. When Clark asked her what she was doing, she candidly responded that she was keeping track of how many words she didn't know on the first page of the book. When they looked at her Post-It, it was dominated with no's rather than yes's. With that, Jordan said, "The book is too hard. There are too many no's on my Post-It." Jordan had internalized this book selection strategy and made it her own. Help your readers do the same.
What can family members/ caregivers do?	Family members and caregivers need to realize that all levels of reading are significant for one reason or another. Help them further understand that their reader needs to be reading books he or she can easily understand. Send home strategies with easy-to-follow explanations so parents can better guide the reading of their children.

Dear family members and caregivers,

We have been talking about making good book choices this week. This is extremely important for young readers, and we need your help.

When children are reading independently they must be reading books that are relatively easy for them. When I see a child return from the library with a book that is obviously too long or too difficult, I see a child holding a book he wishes he could read. Although the goal is to expand book choices for all readers, we must remember that becoming a good reader takes time. There are a few things you can do to help your reader make good book choices:

- Be aware that the books they read independently should not have too many hard words. Although there is no magic number, more than two or three hard words on a page is a signal that the book might be too difficult.

- Be realistic. Most of what we read is easy. Adults, in general, spend more time reading newspapers and magazines than novels.

- Remind your reader that "slow and steady wins the race." Consider a person who is beginning to train with free weights. She would not be wise in choosing 20-lb hand weights on day one. She would probably struggle through the workout and, if not injured, give up because of the intense difficulty. This scenario often happens to children. It is always better to err on the side of too easy than too difficult. We do not want children to give up on reading because they perceive it to be too difficult.

Thank you for helping us grow as readers.

Can It Be For Me?

C = Cover	Look at the cover. Can you gather any information from it?
A = Author	Do you recognize the author's name? Have you read other books by this author?
N = Number of Pages	How long is the book? Does it have too many pages? Does it have too few pages?
I = Illustrations	Does the book include illustrations? Is there an illustration on every page or every few pages?
T = Title or Topic	Do you know anything about the title or topic? Have you heard of the title before?
B = Blurb	What does the blurb tell you about the book? Does it make you want to read more?
E = Entirety	Look at the book in its entirety. Is the print large or small? Are the chapters long or short? And so on.

F = First Impressions	What is your first impression of the book? Does the first line grab your attention? Does the first page capture your interest?
O = Opinions	What do others think about the book? Ask peers and teachers. Look for reviews about the book and awards the book has won.
R = Reverse of the Title Page	Can you find the one-line blurb about the book included with the publication information? It is written in very small print, but will tell you something about the book.
M = My Friends	What do your friends think about the book? Ask them what they think about the book and/or author.
E = Ending	How about reading the last page first? See what it tells you about the book.

Characterization

What do you hear or see?

As a fourth grader comes to the end of a passage he selected to read, you ask him about the character. He supplies you with a beautiful retelling of what he has just read, but provides very little, if any information about the main character. Thinking he must have misunderstood your question, you ask him again to tell you about the main character. He replies, "Well, he is a boy. He is in trouble."

"What else do you know about him?" you ask, hoping he will elaborate. Instead of elaboration, your question is met with a shrug of the shoulders and an unknowing smile.

Why does it matter?

The characters in chapter books, picture books, and poems are often the element of the story that we remember forever. It is true that we might be familiar with a particular setting and we might have had experiences similar to those being written about, but it is the characters we make connections to, form bonds with, and carry with us. Readers of all ages need to know how to understand and appreciate characters for all they're worth.

At times, the reader lives vicariously through the characters in a book. At other times, the character provides insight into the author or illustrator of the book, exploring their hopes, dreams, and hardships. The better you understand a character, the better you can understand, appreciate, and learn from what you are reading.

What do you do?

Comb your classroom, school, or local library for books containing favorite characters. Go with your heart and choose books with characters that are memorable to you. Maybe you could pick some books from your own childhood. To this day, *Petunia* (1977) by Roger Duvoisin is Maryann's favorite children's book. She loves the giddy namesake character of Petunia, the silly goose who thinks she has made herself smart by carrying around a book. Her character is vividly portrayed and becomes stronger at the resolution of the book. Choose books that have memorable, meaningful characters.

Picture books are a wonderful means to get at the heart of characterization, because you are provided with much information in a relatively short period of time. One of our favorite picture book characters is the title character from *The Dinosaurs of Waterhouse Hawkins* (Kerley, 2001). This Caldecott Award honor book is an immediate hit with children of all ages. We have used this biographical picture book to delve deeply into the character of this amazing man and typically spend a week exploring this text.

We begin by using our questioning strategies to pose questions about the text before we read it, while we read it, and after we read it. This book is so visually rich, children have multiple questions from the front and back covers, and end papers alone. After we have questioned the text, we discuss and answer (or attempt to answer) each of our questions. Next, we sort our answers into one of five categories: questions that are answered in the text, answered in our schema, or answered with an inference; questions that need further research; or questions that are impossible to answer.

After we have thoroughly processed the story, we begin to look at the man behind the words. Near the end of our study of the book, we ask the students to write on a sticky note a single word that best describes Waterhouse Hawkins. We talk about strong, specific words as opposed to weaker, more general words like *cool, nice,* and *weird.* As the children come to the circle for discussion, they stick their notes on our easel. We then group similar words, discussing each one. We next begin a collaborative process of elimination, narrowing the word choices down to the three we feel best describe the spirit and essence of Waterhouse Hawkins. After this experience, the kids never look at characters the same way again.

A favorite chapter book of ours is Katherine Paterson's poignant *Bridge to Terabithia* (1977). This Newbery Award-winning classic is full of well-written, intriguing characters. This story of a boy searching for his identity as he befriends a girl from circumstances very different than his own relies upon a sturdy foundation of memorable characters. The main characters of this book are beautifully presented in the first two chapters. Along with the supporting characters, they come together to weave a story that is unforgettable to all who read it.

What can the reader do independently and collaboratively?

- Have students keep a classroom chart of memorable characters they come across in their reading. Older students may want to keep a data sheet with the same information in their literature log.
- While reading a chapter book, have children sketch or draw what they imagine a character looks like. Our own imaginations are always better than the very best computer animation available. It is always interesting to see how the children's illustrations, based on descriptions from the book, are similar, yet so different. If reading a picture book with a memorable character, read it without showing the illustrations. Have the class draw the character as they see him in their mind's eye. Mo Willems's book, *Leonardo, the Terrible Monster* (2005), would work well for this lesson. Several friendly monster-style characters are described.
- Consider hosting a "Favorite Book Character Day" in your classroom, your grade level, or your school. Be forewarned: Family members and caregivers may bemoan such an idea. But, with careful planning, thoughtful directions, and plenty of time, the event is bound to be a success. Children might dress as their favorite character or bring an assortment of items relating to their favorite character. Don't be surprised if you have cartoon and action hero-type characters show up for the event. Some teachers may not consider these characters as *real* characters of children's literature.

However, the research of Tom Newkirk (2002) suggests that indulging boys' fascination with action hero characters actually supports their literacy development.

What can family members/ caregivers do? Have family members and caregivers discuss favorite characters with their children. Often, these characters and the books they come from evoke strong memories.

Dear family members and caregivers,

We have enjoyed reading about and discussing some very interesting characters this week. If you are like us, we bet you have some favorite movie, television, and book characters yourselves. Understanding the reasons why our character behaves as he or she does is an important part of reading. You can help in several ways:

- Share your current favorite characters with your reader. What makes him or her one of your favorites?

- Share your favorite storybook character from childhood. Many adults have fond memories of a teacher who read aloud to them. Is there a character that comes to mind?

- Tell your reader family stories that involve interesting people. These people are the characters of our lives and are fun to share.

- Ask your reader about the characters we are discussing at school. You don't have to know too much about the book to talk to your reader about it. Ask questions like: Do you like the character? Why do you like/dislike the character? Would you like to have this character visit? Does the character make the story better?

Thank you for helping us grow as readers.

Context Clues: Antonyms

What do you hear or see?

While analyzing the results of a recent reading assessment you note that many of your students consistently miss inferential questions. Upon closer examination of the complete assessment, you notice that most of the students missed the definition of a key word when the word was surrounded by obvious antonyms and contrasting examples. It is not their inability to define the word that troubles you, it was their inability to use the clues in the text to infer the meaning of the word. You determine that your class needs to explore context clues that involve the use of antonyms.

Why does it matter?

Often, nonexamples of a word or concept help cement our understanding. It is sometimes critical to understand what something is *not* before we can truly understand what it *is*. We begin teaching children about antonyms in preschool. Children often spend a great deal of time in the primary grades putting together antonym puzzles and matching pictures that show opposite meanings. We agree that an understanding of antonyms is important; however, we believe that it is the application of this knowledge that truly matters. Children must use this understanding to decipher context clues that are rooted in antonyms and contrasting information. Why is understanding antonyms so important? When applied to the context of reading, it can deepen comprehension.

What do you do?

Model how you use antonyms to help you construct meaning for challenging words. Use authentic text examples to show children that authors use words and phrases like *but, however, instead, although,* and *even though* as clues that antonyms for the hard word are about to follow.

In *Arrowhawk*, Lola M. Schaefer (2004) uses both a cue and an antonym to help the reader understand the word *remote*.

> He searched for a remote tree to perch, but all he saw were buildings, cars, and people.

The word *but* is a signal that an antonym clue, or in this case, several antonym clues are about to follow. Although buildings, cars, and people are not direct antonyms for the word *remote,* they do provide information about what is *not* remote.

We have also found that *Kids Discover* magazines contain many examples of antonym context clues. One interesting issue, *Garbage*, has particularly strong examples. On page 15 an antonym clue is used to help children understand the job of a garbologist:

> Called garbologists, these scientists study garbage for what it can teach us about human behavior. Most were trained to be archaeologists, scientists who study prehistoric peoples and their way of life. However, instead of studying peoples of the distant past, garbologists look at garbage for what it can tell us about people's lives today.

The word *however* cues the reader that an antonym context clue is forthcoming. Although the word garbologist is defined in the passage, the reader is offered more information when this occupation is contrasted with that of an archeologist.

What can the reader do independently and collaboratively?	• Ask readers to use the "Using Antonym Clues" chart included at the end of this lesson to keep track of context clues in their independent texts.
	• Encourage readers to share their context clue monitoring charts. Listening to others discuss how they recognized the context clue will benefit readers who are struggling to do so.

Using Antonym Clues

Book _____

Genre _____

New word and page number	Cue that antonyms were coming	Antonyms given in the text for the new word

Context Clues:
Descriptions and Examples

**What do you
hear or see?**

While discussing Robert San Souci's *Kate Shelley Bound for Legend* (1995), you are stunned that the students have not grasped the essence of her. She did, after all, risk her life to save people she thought were in danger. Sure, maybe they don't know what the word *heroine* means, but the book was full of rich description. How could they miss it?

**Why does
it matter?**

Context clues are vital tools that lead to rich comprehension. As readers grow into early chapter books and then into novels, they rely less and less on picture support and instead rely more on the context of the story to construct meaning. Within the story are word clues, also called *context clues,* that support this building of meaning. Although we tend to think of context clues in general terms, there are several specific types of context clues that readers must be aware of. A cursory mention of context clues is not enough. Students need to explore context clues and be able to identify them in their reading. In fiction, the author will often provide a description of a challenging word or concept. In nonfiction, authors tend to include specific examples.

**What do
you do?**

You must model for children how you use descriptive context clues and example context clues. In our experience, this requires two separate lessons, because descriptive clues are more often found in the language of narrative text and example clues are more often found in expository text.

The example clues are generally easier to spot and are therefore probably the best place to start. Several words and phrases are *cues* that alert us that example clues are to follow: *for example, such as, including*, and *like*. You can typically find examples with these cue words in any nonfiction trade book or textbook.

Gail Gibbons is an author of nonfiction who infuses her books with all forms of context clues. An excerpt from *Catch the Wind! All About Kites* (1989) demonstrates the use of example clues.

> Kites can be made from many different materials, including paper, cloth, plastic, nylon, and Mylar.

Descriptive clues are more subtle and require children to make connections and inferences. We have had great success using Allen Say's *Emma's Rug* (2005a) to think aloud through our process of using descriptive context clues to analyze the actions and spirit of the title character. The main character, Emma, erroneously believes that her vivid imagination and uncanny artistic ability are somehow connected to a rug. This rug, given to her as an infant, has become her source of comfort and security. When her unwitting mother washes her rug, Emma is distraught. She fears that the source of her inspiration is ruined. Eventually she realizes that the true source of her art is her own imagination. In this beautifully descriptive book, students use multiple clues from the context to analyze Emma's emotions.

What can the reader do independently and collaboratively?

- When reading nonfiction independently, encourage students to identify example clues and the cues that alerted them to their presence.
- During a writer's workshop, conduct a minilesson about the importance of including example clues and their cues in nonfiction pieces. This will empower the student to use these clues independently as both a reader and a writer.
- When students are attempting to analyze a character's actions or emotions, ask them to jot down the words the author uses to describe the character. These descriptive clues are helpful when attempting to make generalizations about a character.
- Have small groups of students read texts that include rich descriptive clues and analyze the motives, actions, or emotions of the characters. Ask the students to provide specific examples from the text that support their conclusion.
- After conducting a model reading lesson with *Emma's Rug*, extend the experience to writer's workshop. This lesson further illustrates the importance of using descriptive words as a writer. This will encourage students to use such language as they write independently.

Using Example Clues

Book _____

Genre _____

New word and page number	Cue that examples were coming	Examples given in the text

Context Clues: Synonyms

What do you hear or see?

While conferring with a student, she enthusiastically tells you all about the Loch Ness monster. You glance down at the text and notice the word *verify* in heavy, dark letters. Curious to see if she understands this word, you ask if anyone has been able to verify the existence of Nessie. Not sure of your question, she asks for clarification. Even though the word *prove* follows the word *verify* in the text, the reader has been unable to use this synonym to construct meaning. You determine that this student needs to explore context clues that involve the use of synonyms.

Why does it matter?

In most cases, the writer of a text does not set out to confound, but actually works hard to ensure that his or her reader understands the intended message. Along with other types of context clues authors often attempt to define concepts and words for their readers without explicitly stating a definition. They sometimes include words with similar meanings or synonyms to clarify the meaning of a word.

What do you do?

As with all forms of context clues, it is critical that students explore their use in works of both fiction and nonfiction. This form of context clue appears often in content-specific text. Consider the following sample from *Sweeping Tsunamis* by Louise and Richard Spillsbury (2005, 4):

> As ocean waves move into shallow water, their narrow foaming tips curl over and "break," or collapse. A tsunami hits land as a dark, fast moving ledge of water that rarely breaks as it nears shore.

By examining this sample it becomes clear that *tsunami* is, at least in part, a synonym for the word *wave*, because the word *break* is used to describe them both. The words *curl over* and *collapse* are synonyms for the word *break*.

Synonyms are more likely to connect with the prior knowledge of the reader, thus enhancing his or her understanding of the questionable word. We encourage you to examine examples of synonym context clues and discuss the use and purpose of the words in each.

We have used excerpts from Richard Peck's *A Year Down Yonder* (2000, 22; an excellent read-aloud for all ages) to explore this form of context clue in fiction. Using chart paper or an overhead projector, reproduce an appropriate excerpt so it is large enough to be seen by all. The book contains several good examples, but you might try the following passage:

> Being fifteen, I didn't tell Grandma any more about high school than I could help. But she always knew everything anyway, so I showed her a notice from the principal, Mr. Fluke. The grammar in it was good, so Miss Butler must have ghostwritten it. She asked parents to provide party refreshments. In those times people turned out in droves if there was anything to eat.
>   "Vittles," Grandma said, scanning Miss Butler's appeal. "That'll mean pies."

The word *vittles* is not one common to most of our students, but the definition of the word is deftly hidden in the text. By identifying and highlighting clues to the meaning of the word *vittles,* children will engage in analyzing the words *refreshments, anything to eat,* and *pie.* Although some might erroneously initially believe that vittles actually means pies, closer examination and discussion about our connections to the word *refreshments* has left our students understanding that vittles (actually a nonstandard form of the word *victuals*) is another word for food.

For an example of a synonym clue used in poetry take a look at "An Eye" in Doug Florian's *Bing, Bang, Boing* (1996).

> An eye for an eye, a tooth for a tooth. Sticking your tongue out is rude and uncouth.

In this short poem, the word *rude* is used as a synonym for uncouth, a word that is not likely to be in the schema of most children.

What can the reader do independently and collaboratively?

- Ask the readers to use the synonym clue chart included at the end of this lesson to list the definitional context clues in their independent texts.
- Encourage readers to share their context clue monitoring charts. Listening to others discuss how they recognized the context clue will benefit readers who are struggling to do so.

Using Synonym Clues

Book_____

Genre _____

New word and page number	Synonyms for the new word	Meaning of the new word given in the text

Context Clues: Definitions

What do you hear or see?

When conferring with a child about an article in *National Geographic Explorer*, you notice the word *regurgitates* in bold print near the bottom of the page. You cannot resist the urge to inquire about the meaning of that word. The reader explains that penguin mothers regurgitate food for their chicks to eat. You continue to push, asking what the word actually means. The reader looks at you, shrugs and says, "I guess it means to feed a baby." You are a little surprised by this lack of understanding. The word is clearly defined in the sentences that follow. Does this child understand how to use definitional context clues?

Why does it matter?

Context clues are vital tools that lead to rich comprehension. As readers grow into early chapter books and then into novels, they rely less and less on picture support and instead rely on the context of the story to construct meaning. Within the story are word clues, also called *context clues,* that support this building of meaning. Although we tend to think of context clues in general terms, there are several specific types of context clues that readers must be aware of because students need to explore context clues and be able to identify them in their reading. A good starting point for most readers is to work with context clues that are definitional in nature and explain the meaning of words and phrases. Sometimes this definition is explicitly stated and sometimes the word is simply restated in simpler terms. This type of context clue is common in most genres, but is key to understanding nonfiction.

What do you do?

Introduce the idea of context clues to your class during a shared reading. An anchor chart that states a simple definition and purpose for using context clues will keep the children focused on the importance of using them to become better "comprehenders" of text.

Follow this experience with a similar lesson that focuses on definitional context clues. We recommend a shared reading experience with an oversize nonfiction text. Many good choices are available at various levels, but we have enjoyed working with the Heinemann science series. Prior to the lesson, select a page or two that includes a word in bold type followed by the definition of the word. The lesson will be more beneficial if you select a content-specific word for which the children have limited background knowledge. This will require the readers to rely more on the context than their schema. In the book *Screws* by Angela Royston (2001), many key words are clearly and succinctly defined. For example, on page 5, the word *screw* is defined as "a simple machine," and on page 25, the word *propeller* is defined as "a kind of screw."

The presence of the verb "to be" also signals that the definition of the word is upcoming. After reading a text together, discuss possible meanings of the boldface word. As the children offer possible meanings, urge them to take their thinking to a higher level by asking them *why* they are thinking what they are thinking. What clues in the text led them to a definition for the word? How was the clue helpful?

This lesson must be repeated using a fictional text. One good example is found in Kate DiCamillo's *Because of Winn-Dixie* (2000, 75). Using chart paper or the overhead projector, reproduce excerpts that model the use of definitional context clues. The following excerpt clearly illustrates the lesson.

> "Opal?" said the preacher. He was lying on his stomach, and Winn-Dixie was sitting on top of him, panting and whining.
> "Yes, sir," I said.
> "Opal," the preacher said again.
> "Yes, sir," I said louder.
> "Do you know what a pathological fear is?"
> "No, sir," I told him.
> The preacher raised a hand. He rubbed his nose. "Well," he said, after a minute, "It's a fear that goes way beyond normal fears. It's a fear you can't be talked out of or reasoned out of."

After reading the text, the students identified "it's" as the contraction for "it is," thus recognizing the presence of the "be" verb. They were then able to recognize the definition of a pathological fear.

Another good example can be found in an excerpt from another one of our favorites, Eve Bunting's *Smoky Night* (1994b).

> Mama and I stand well back from our window, looking down. I'm holding Jasmine, my cat. We don't have our lights on though it's almost dark. People are rioting in the streets below.
> Mama explains about rioting, "It can happen when people get angry. They want to smash and destroy. They don't care anymore what's right and what's wrong."
> Below us they are smashing everything. Windows, cars, streetlights.

We recommend copying the text onto large chart paper, highlighting the unknown words (*pathological fear* and *rioting*), the "be" verbs (when applicable), and identifying the definition of the word.

What can the reader do independently and collaboratively?

- Ask the readers to list the definitional context clues in their independent texts on the Using Definition Clues chart included at the end of this lesson.
- Encourage readers to share their context clue monitoring charts. Listening to others discuss how they recognized the context clue will benefit readers who are struggling to do so.

Using Definition Clues

Book _____

Genre _____

New word and page number	Cue that a definition was coming	Definition for the new word given in the text

Context Clues:
Inferring Word Meaning

What do you hear or see?

While reading *Snowflake Bentley* (Martin, 1998) to a group of third grade students, you notice that several students are confounded by the fact that William Bentley tries to draw snowflakes inside his house. Didn't the book tell us that he grew up in Vermont where it snows an average of 120 inches each year? You would think he knew something about snow. What was this guy thinking? Yes, these are children in the Deep South who do not often experience snow, but they do know that snow melts when the temperature rises above freezing. He should just move his microscope outside and draw them there. End of story!

When reflecting on this observation you realize that the students have failed to infer some critical information. You decide to think aloud through your process of understanding this single page of text, pointing out the specific clues that guide your thinking.

Why does it matter?

Inferring is key to comprehending text. Harvey and Goudvis (2000) have identified inferring as one of several comprehension strategies that proficient readers employ. Simply put, clues from the text must be melded with information in the reader's schema in order for inferring to occur. Although some teachers believe that children develop the ability to infer naturally, we believe this to be a dangerous assumption. Generalizing and inferring must be modeled and discussed.

What do you do?

After reading *Snowflake Bentley* aloud to your class, examine the following page of the text carefully. As William Bentley explored the world of snowflakes, the story tells us that,

> Their intricate patterns were even more beautiful than he had imagined. He expected to find whole flakes that were the same, that were copies of each other. But he never did. Willie decided there must be a way to save snowflakes so others could see their wonderful designs. For three winters he tried drawing snow crystals. They always melted before he could finish.

The word *intricate* is likely to be a word that is not in the vocabularies of many students and is key to inferring the reasons behind some of Bentley's actions. By thinking about what the word *intricate* describes (patterns) and looking closely at the other words used to describe the crystals (wonderful designs), we can arrive at a working definition for "intricate" that will allow us to discuss this word thoroughly. When this learning is accompanied by the additional text on the page, the word becomes even more clear.

> He learned that most crystals had six branches (though a few had three). For each snowflake the six branches were alike. "I found that snowflakes were masterpieces of design," he said. "No one design was ever repeated. When a snowflake melted . . . just that much beauty was gone, without leaving any record behind."

The word *design* appears in this passage. Near this word we see the word *masterpieces*. Discuss your own understanding of the word *masterpieces* and allow the students to do likewise. What is a masterpiece? How are masterpieces created? How long does it take to create a masterpiece? Can a masterpiece ever be recreated?

We also learn that most crystals have six identical branches. The illustrator shows us these branches. You note that they look complex. How long would it take to draw six identical branches? Would it be easy to draw a complex snowflake? Would it be easy to draw an intricate snowflake with thick gloves on your hands? Would it be easy to draw snowflakes with shaking hands that were exposed to bitter cold?

By modeling your own thinking with this single page of text, students will probably infer what our third grade friends inferred. Snowflakes are so intricate and complicated that Bentley wouldn't have been able to draw them with the thick wool gloves (shown in the illustration) on his hands. Gloves would make it difficult for Bentley to do his drawing outside. Drawing the snowflakes would take such a long time he would surely get a case of frostbite. Suddenly, the kids are rooting for William Bentley because their inferences have led them to appreciate fully the challenge that he faces.

What can the reader do independently and collaboratively?

- Record inferences in reading journals and share specific words (context clues) that prompted the thinking.
- Participate in literature discussion groups that regularly discuss their inferences and the thinking behind them.

Dear family members and caregivers,

We have been talking about context clues and how they help us understand what we read. Context clues are word clues that authors put in text to help us understand difficult words and concepts. Although we are learning how to recognize and use context clues, it will take time for your reader to be able to use them efficiently.

Think about the following: *The egregious mistake was horrible and irresponsible.* In this sentence, the word egregious is somewhat unfamiliar. Although you may or may not be able to pronounce the word correctly, you have a good idea about what the word *egregious* means. You just used context clues!

You can help your reader practice using context clues in several ways.

- Resist the temptation to tell your reader to "sound out" difficult words, because this strategy is actually not very effective. Instead, ask, "What word would make sense there?" If your reader is unable to answer that question, tell him or her to "read on." Sometimes context clues are prior to the difficult word, but other times they come after it.

- Remember, being able to pronounce a word correctly is not as important as knowing what the word means. Ask, "Are there any clues that can help you understand what the word means?"

Thank you for helping us grow as readers.

Contractions

What do you hear or see?

While taking a running record, you notice that the reader substitutes both words for common contractions and mispronounces other, less common contractions altogether. Every time she encountered the word *we're* she said *were*.

Why does it matter?

Substituting both words in the place of a contraction does not affect the meaning of the text being read and is only problematic when reading accuracy is being analyzed. When contractions are mispronounced, however, it can impede understanding and must be addressed.

What do you do?

If the purpose for reading is to make meaning from print, we are not so certain that anything must be done when students substitute two words in the place of a contraction. Substitutions that reflect active comprehension and self-monitoring actually make us very happy. Unfortunately, some assessments today place extreme emphasis on accuracy and speed in reading. In such cases, teachers are compelled to call such miscues to the attention of their students. Often, taking the reader back to the text to reflect upon the miscue is enough. This can provide additional insight into the reasons for the miscue. Was the reader thrown off by the mere presence of an apostrophe? Was the contraction one that the reader does not often encounter?

We have observed that students frequently struggle with contractions that involve the verbs "have" and "had" (should've, could've, she'd, I'd, we'd). Could it be that these are contractions that are a part of the reader's spoken vocabulary, but occur so infrequently in text that he or she does not recognize them in print?

Contractions must be explicitly taught. We model the use of contractions in oral language constantly, yet we sometimes urge children not to use them in their writing. Contractions have been labeled "informal" and are typically present only in the dialogue of a text. We must explicitly show children how these spoken words look, and encourage them to use contractions in their writing. A chart of contractions and their correspondences might be posted in the classroom.

What can the reader do independently and collaboratively?	• Ask the reader to identify contractions during independent reading. These contractions can be recorded and discussed during individual conferences and added to the aforementioned contractions chart.
	• Take a contractions scavenger hunt through a newspaper or magazine article, highlighting each contraction. Compare the words highlighted, searching for contractions that might be new to the students.
	• Encourage the use of contractions during independent writing.
	• Let readers attempt to match contractions and their correspondences in a collaborative setting (see reproducible).

What can family members/ caregivers do?	• Listen and provide appropriate, supportive feedback.
	• Model the use of contractions in speech.
	• Play a game in which you challenge the reader to be "contraction free" for a set period of time. The reader will search his memory for correspondences each time he recalls a contraction.

Contraction Concentration

Cut along the dotted lines.

can't	can not	I'd	I would
aren't	are not	she'll	she will
I'll	I will	you'll	you will
should've	should have	won't	will not
he'll	he will	I've	I have
would've	would have	it'll	it will
we're	we are	we've	we have

Contraction Concentration

Cut along the dotted lines.

we'll	we will	we'd	we would
they're	they are	they've	they have
they'll	they will	doesn't	does not
don't	do not	he'd	he would
she'd	she would	I'm	I am
isn't	is not	here's	here is
who'll	who will	who'd	who would

Dialogue

What do you hear or see?

Dialogue breathes life into the characters we read about. Dialogue provides the reader with a deeper understanding of the characters themselves. Even young children seem to understand that quotation marks, or talking marks as they simplistically refer to them, denote lines or sections of text where someone is speaking. At times, dialogue is easy for the reader to follow and at others it can be quite complicated, especially if there are myriad characters involved. Often a reader will come to you with an exasperated feeling, telling you that they have lost track of who is speaking. Of course, when this confusion occurs, comprehension is greatly impeded.

Why does it matter?

Understanding how to read dialogue between characters is critical to the success of any age reader. The conversations characters have help shape their personas just as the conversations we have in life. Similar to body language, our conversations, both spoken and written, shape who we are.

What do you do?

- Search for examples of dialogue in varying difficulties. Some dialogue is written so that it is easily followed. Each phrase is accompanied by the appropriate identifier. As the degree of difficulty in dialogue increases, these identifiers become less frequent.
- Make an example of dialogue when you come to it in shared, guided and read-aloud reading. Demonstrate by thinking aloud how you deal with dialogue that is both easy and difficult to follow. You might make a brief statement such as, "This conversation is easy to follow. The author clearly tells me who is speaking" with easier dialogue. Demonstrate your thinking process as you come across more challenging dialogue that is harder to follow: "I have lost track of who is speaking. I am confused and need to go back to the point in the conversation where I know who was speaking."
- Explain to readers that following dialogue is similar to following a tennis match. Sometimes the match is between just two people, but sometimes four (or more for that matter) are involved. The more people speaking, the more closely you have to pay attention to who is saying what.
- Use varying degrees of dialogue as examples. Interesting dialogue appears in Jennifer L. Holm's 1999 Newbery honor award-winning book, *Our Only Mae Ameilia*. Holm doesn't use quotation marks at all to distinguish which character is speaking making the reader pay extra close attention. Sharon Creech makes creative use of font styles in the *The Wanderer*, a Newbery honor award-winning book from 2001. In this book, each character is denoted by a unique font from chapter to chapter to help the reader keep track of whose voice they are reading.

- Use highlighter pens of varying colors or highlighting tape to color code a selected piece of conversation in a book. At a glance, readers will be able to practice determining which character is speaking.

What can the reader do independently and collaboratively?

- Caution readers that if something is said that doesn't seem to fit the character they believe is speaking, that this may be a warning well heeded. They may quite possibly have lost the flow of the dialogue.
- Make sure readers know the importance of going back to where they were following the flow of dialogue should their comprehension break down.
- Encourage readers to compare and contrast written conversation with oral conversation; discussing their thinking in small groups.
- Books on tape are helpful for readers of all abilities as they seek to make sense of dialogue.

Dear family members and caregivers,

We have been paying particular attention to the dialogue we encountered in the books we have been reading. We have discovered that dialogue plays a very important role in telling a story. It can also be difficult to follow. Here are some quick ideas to help your reader interact successfully with dialogue:

- Be aware of dialogue when you are reading with your child. Make sure they understand that dialogue can be quite challenging to follow and subsequently comprehend. Should you come across any interesting examples of dialogue, please send them in so they can be discussed with the class. Maybe another meaning-ensuring strategy will emerge from your example.

- Look for examples of varying degrees of dialogue in the texts you are reading with your child. These examples could then be incorporated into the dialogue continuum being used and discussed in class.

Thank you for helping us grow as readers.

Foreign Phrases

Dee-
D-

Miscue: The man shouted "De-us vult" (God wills it) as he fell off the slope.
s-see-
      The girl said "S'il vous plait" (If you please) to the waiter when he offered her water.

What do you hear or see?

While listening to a student read, you notice that he attempts to decode a foreign phrase sound by sound. After trying for several seconds, the child tells you that he thinks the book is too difficult.

Why does it matter?

No amount of decoding will help a student understand the meaning of a foreign phrase. The amount of time and energy spent attempting to "sound out" these words will impede understanding.

What do you do?

Discuss the purpose of foreign phrases in text with your students. They add a layer of interest to text that is culturally rich and linguistically pleasing. They also expose children to elements of languages they may some day study.

You must also talk to children about the best way to handle these phrases. In almost all cases, foreign phrases are easily identifiable because they are printed in italics. We have also discovered that these italicized phrases are almost always translated into English immediately following the phrases. One of our favorite authors, Pam Ryan peppers her novels *Esperanza Rising* (2000) and *Becoming Naomi Leon* (2005) with Spanish phrases. Knowing little Spanish, we have noticed that we tend to skip the Spanish phrases initially and read on to find Pam's translation, which we know is coming. Our eyes skip to the translation first, and then retrace the text to associate the words we know to the words we don't. For example, on page 146 of *Becoming Naomi Leon*, the words "¡Hola! !Aqui estamos!" grab our attention. First, there are punctuation marks that we do not readily recognize, and second, the words are in italics. These words are followed by "We are here." Using our schema (we actually know that *hola* means hello) we are able to construct that this phrase means, "Hello. We are here."

You might also make a transparency of a page or two from *Sam and the Lucky Money* by Karen Chinn (1999). In this book, Chinese phrases are easily identified and translated. After placing the transparency on the overhead, ask a student to underline the foreign phrases in one color and the translation in another. For older readers, any page from

Gail Carson Levine's *Ella Enchanted* (1997) that includes phrases written in the fictional language of Ogrese will also serve the same purpose. Emphasize that pronouncing the phrase correctly is unimportant. It is the translation that matters. Although we stop short of telling kids to skip over foreign phrases, we do encourage them to focus on the translations first.

What can the reader do independently and collaboratively?	• Encourage the reader to highlight the translations of foreign phrases. This encourages a focus on meaning.
	• Many word processing programs contain a translation command. Demonstrate how to use this tool and encourage children to try it. They could type the foreign phrases into the computer and read the translation.
	• Ask kids to keep a list of the foreign phrases they encounter. These can be discussed during share time.

Foreign Vocabulary

Miscue: The young man was overjoyed when he won the scholarship, but he couldn't decide whether to study at (Cambridge) or the (Sorbonne.)

What do you hear or see?

While listening to the children make their lunch choices, you notice a commotion beside the day's lunch menu. The kids are attempting to read the day's lunch choices with little success. They are growing increasingly agitated, so you decide to intervene. You can't help but smile when you see the day's choices: a ham and cheese croissant or a chicken fajita. You decide that second grade is not too early for a talk about words we encounter that originated in other places.

Why does it matter?

Children will encounter foreign vocabulary often in fiction as well as functional text. We differentiate foreign vocabulary from foreign phrases because, unlike phrases, single words like cologne are often not set off by italics. Although some of these words are common in our spoken language, others are not. Kids are caught off guard and often waste good cognitive energy trying to decode words like croissant and fajita. Although many words are actually the names of foods, others like futon and beret are not.

Many consider the language of technology a foreign language. In some institutions, proficiency in the language of computing is considered mastery of a second language. Words like RAM, ROM, Google, and Wikipedia are now part of not only the English language, but a global language that is understood across cultures.

Our purpose is to build an awareness of foreign vocabulary and an interest in the languages and cultures that have added these words to our vocabularies. Sometimes these words are italicized and thus alert the reader that the word might be a challenge. Others make no distinction between the foreign word and words more familiar to the reader.

What do you do?

Seek out books that include foreign vocabulary. Be sure to include as many languages and cultures as possible. For example, Chris Raschka's *Arlene Sardine* (1998) is brimming with interesting words such as *brisling, hermetically sealed,* and *purse net.* It also exposes kids to the word *fjord,* a word that came to us by way of Scandanavia. *Big Moon Tortilla* by Joy Cowley (1998) contains a Spanish word (*tortilla*) in both the title and text that kids are very familiar with. By looking closely at two words that came to us from two different countries, kids can begin to make generalizations about the sounds that letters make in different languages. In the examples *fjord* and *tortilla*, /y/ is expressed by differing symbols. Although we do not advocate teaching children the phonetic rules for each and every foreign word they encounter, we do think it is a good idea to show children that most words aren't decodable to us because they follow a very different set of rules. We encourage children to treat these words like they treat challenging names. Make a guess and move on. The important thing is to try and understand what the word means.

Because the use of foreign vocabulary varies from region to region and town to town, we have found environmental print, cookbooks, newspapers, and menus to be excellent print resources for exploring foreign words. A quick tour of your town or neighborhood might reveal more foreign words on store fronts and billboards than you expected. Snap a picture and discuss the words you see. In our experience, families and caregivers have been happy to share recipes for family dishes that reveal delicious words like *andouille, lutefisk, chapiti,* and *gnocci*. Restaurateurs will often share copies of menus with your class. Happily, many even include pronunciation guides. If not, Ted Lewin's *Big Jimmy's Kum Kau Chinese Take Out* (2002) contains an illustrated menu on the end papers.

What can the reader do independently and collaboratively?

Foreign vocabulary abounds. Encourage your students always to be on the lookout for it. Ask them to jot down foreign words they encounter during their reading so they can share them with the class. Use the context to determine the word's meaning. Add the word and meaning to the class chart. When words are found multiple times, this indicates the word is one we need to know. We indicate multiple encounters with a word with tally marks beside it on our chart.

Our favorite books that include foreign words and phrases include

Big Moon Tortilla by Joy Cowley (1998)
Arlene Sardine by Chris Raschka (1998)
A Day's Work by Eve Bunting (1994a)
Sam and the Lucky Money by Karen Chinn (1999)
Kamishibai Man by Allen Say (2005b)
Frida Maria by Deborah Nourse Lattimore (1994)
Manana Iguana by Ann Whitford Paul (2004)
Mercedes and the Chocolate Pilot by Margot Theis Raven (2002)
The Sweetest Fig by Chris Van Allsburg (1993)
Kira Kira by Cynthia Kodahata (2004)
The Outcasts of 19 Schuyler Place by E. L. Konigsburg (2004)

Dear family members and caregivers,

We have been talking about foreign words and phrases and strategies for reading them. Foreign words and phrases are common in books and the environment. It is important for children to know how to handle them.

Foreign phrases in books are often written in italics. This signals the reader that the phrase is written in a language other than English. We have discussed that these phrases are often followed by an English translation in the text. For example, on page 146 of *Becoming Naomi Leon* (a book we are reading in class), the words *"¡Hola! ¡Aquí estamos!"* grab our attention. First, there are punctuation marks that we do not readily recognize, and second, the words are in italics. These words are followed by "We are here." Using our prior knowledge (we actually know that *hola* means hello), we are able to figure out that this phrase means, "Hello. We are here."

Many foreign words are now part of our spoken and written language: cologne, futon, tortilla, fajita. They are not usually written in italics and cannot be "sounded out." In this case, tell your reader how to pronounce the word and remind him or her to look for clues to help understand what the word means.

You can help by

- Reminding your reader not to "sound out" foreign words and phrases. It is a better use of energy to look for clues about meaning.

Thank you for helping us grow as readers.

Hyphenated Words

What do you hear or see?

While listening to a child read aloud, you notice that she actually says the word "dash" when reading the words that describe a "3000-acre landfill." She says the word "dash" again when the word "samples" is broken between syllables and hyphenated. Hyphenated words occur when a word needs to be divided between syllables at the end of a line and to modify words themselves. *The Chicago Manual of Style* (2003) states, "In general, a compound modifier comprising an adjective plus a noun and preceding the word or words it modifies should be hyphenated." Children need a minilesson that addresses hyphenated words.

Why does it matter?

Understanding hyphenated words is critical to building meaning. This is especially true as text becomes increasingly longer and more complicated to comprehend.

What do you do?

Share with readers the two ways in which hyphenated words are used, and remind them that hyphens are clues to readers that have no corresponding sound. Older students will undoubtedly come across more hyphenated words in their reading than younger students. Of course, with a younger child you may choose to provide a less concise example than the one provided by the *Chicago Manual of Style*. In general, a younger student's reading will consist mainly of words hyphenated at the end of a line rather than words in which an adjective and noun come before the word they modify. With any age student, a discussion about hyphenated words provides a natural segue into another lesson about the rules of syllabication.

What can the reader do independently and collaboratively?

Practice dividing words at the end of the line when writing. We have all reminded children that letters crammed together at the very edge of the page are often difficult for the reader to understand. We have found that once children are introduced to hyphens, they are happy to use them. You might find yourself conducting a minilesson about the overuse of hyphens!

Idiomatic Expressions and Figures of Speech

What do you hear or see?

During independent reading, a student in your class appears before you with a look of utter confusion. She is a strong reader, and this look is not one you have ever seen before. She holds before you her current book about Helen Keller and says, "It says in here that Helen was the apple of her mother's eye. How in the world can Helen be an apple?" The two of you can't help but laugh. It is time to have a talk about idioms.

Why does it matter?

Idioms are a part of our language. Simply put, idioms do not mean what they actually say. They are rooted in social knowledge and are understood by the speakers of a language; however, if misunderstood, they can be alarming. Some more regionally specific idioms are a part of our spoken vocabularies, whereas others that are more general appear often in text. How many of us have actually seen a child look down at his pants when someone asks if "he has money burning a hole in his pocket." Although idiomatic expressions have always been troublesome for young readers who have difficulty making the literal abstract, they are particularly difficult for English language learners.

Idioms are often used as descriptive context clues. Consider the previous example. If the reader does not understand the meaning of the idiom "apple of my eye," she will fail to comprehend that Helen's mother loved her greatly. Without support from someone who understands the expression, the reader might go on believing, as this reader initially thought, that Helen was a McIntosh apple somehow lodged in her mother's eye.

What do you do?

First, reflect on your use of idiomatic expressions. Research and experience tells us that children need multiple experiences with new words before they truly become part of that child's spoken and written vocabulary. We believe the same must be true for idioms because they are highly expressive. Use them when you talk to your class.

Second, read and discuss books that contain idioms. To the delight of his readers, Richard Peck uses figurative language and idiomatic expressions liberally in *The Teacher's Funeral: A Comedy in Three Parts* (2004). From common colloquialisms like "hit pay dirt" and "doctors bury their mistakes" to more unusual ones like "she was all wool and no embroidery," Peck provides us with a bounty of idiomatic expressions to explore with readers. After the definition of an idiom has been discussed and examples given, a read-aloud of this book could serve as an opportunity for students to listen for idioms. We have colleagues whose students have a memo book and pencil in hand as they listen to a read-aloud. In this memo book they jot down questions, interesting words, examples of figurative language, and idioms. They take time each day to discuss their discoveries and wonderings.

What can the reader do independently and collaboratively?

- Ask students to take note of idioms they hear as you read aloud or note ones they encounter as they read independently. Write them down and discuss their meanings.
- Idioms often create a mental image in our minds. Visual idiom dictionaries are available, but we suggest that your students work collaboratively to make their own. As children find idioms in their reading, have them look them up in either the *Scholastic Dictionary of Idioms* (1998) or on one of several websites. When children know the definition, have them illustrate the literal meaning but write the implied meaning on a piece of paper. Place the definitions in sheet protectors in a three-ring binder. This allows for easy reorganization, because the student-made visual dictionary should always be a work in progress.
- Encourage students to use idioms in their writing of fiction, especially in pieces that are intended to be humorous.
- Suggest that your students talk to parents, caregivers, and friends of all ages, and collect interesting idioms from their experience.

Dear family members and caregivers,

We have been talking about idioms and figures of speech. Idioms are phrases that do not actually mean what they say. Some examples you may be familiar with are

- Money burning a hole in your pocket

- Making a mountain out of a molehill

- Bull in a china shop

- Taking the bull by the horns

As books become more difficult, idioms and figures of speech become more common. Because these phrases do not mean what they literally say, they can be confusing to your reader.

You can help by

- Using idioms and figures of speech when you talk to your reader. Don't forget to explain what the sayings actually mean. If you aren't sure what they mean yourself, there are several good idiom dictionaries available both online and at your library.

- Sharing your favorite idioms with us. Many idioms and figures of speech are regionally or culturally specific. You may be able to share new ones with the class.

- Reminding your reader to write down idioms and figures of speech they find as they read. We can explain the meanings and reread the text.

Have fun with idioms and figures of speech!

Thank you for helping us grow as readers.

Ignoring Punctuation

What do you hear or see?

As you listen to a student read, you are impressed by his ability to read fluently. Upon closer inspection, you notice he is completely ignoring one punctuation mark after another. Thankfully, his actions are not consistent, but the miscue happens often enough that it impedes the meaning-making process. After all, you are sure he knows what periods, question marks, exclamation marks, and other marks of punctuation are. You see him demonstrate their use accurately in his writing.

Later in the week, you conduct a reading conference with the same child. You ask the child to read a favorite part of the transitional chapter book he is reading. After thumbing through the pages he has read, the child finally chooses a passage. As you listen, memories of a recent assessment pop to the forefront of your memory. Once again, the child is a seemingly fluent reader; however, he omits key punctuation marks and comprehension is adversely affected. You realize this child needs to attend to punctuation when reading.

Why does it matter?

Punctuation serves a purpose. Without punctuation our thoughts flow together into a stream of incomprehensible, isolated words. Punctuation gives our thoughts the form and structure they need in order for others to understand them. Oftentimes, children demonstrate proficiency of this concept in their own writing much sooner than they do in reading the writing of others. Young children in kindergarten classrooms can tell you a period means to stop and that quotation marks mean someone is talking. We have all seen the overapproximation of this newly constructed knowledge as a young writer ends an exclamatory sentence with a dozen or more exclamation marks. Children who are more concerned with speed and accuracy often ignore punctuation when reading. Omitting these small but very important marks in the name of speed is a costly mistake. Without punctuation, comprehension is almost definitely impeded. If children are to comprehend what they read, we must ensure they understand the importance of punctuation in the writing they read.

What do you do?

- Use a piece of writing that the reader is familiar with and discuss how the meaning depends very much on the punctuation used. Consider the following sentence from Ralph Fletcher's *Fig Pudding* (1995, 51):

  "I'm a free man!" Teddy cried. "A free man!"

If a reader is not paying attention to punctuation he will read the three short sentences as one and may later pose the question: "Why is Teddy crying? He is free." (From his exile of time-out spent underneath the kitchen table.)

- Demonstrate the power of punctuation by typing a familiar passage of text omitting all the punctuation. Show it to students to see if they have a challenging time understanding it. For older students, select a passage with a great deal of dialogue and omit the punctuation and indentations. Students will soon be at a loss and unable to determine which character is speaking.
- Remind the reader that reading and writing share a close relationship. He needs to read like a writer and write like a reader.
- Ensure that the readers in your classroom know that you value understanding over speed.

| **What can the reader do independently and collaboratively?** | • Encourage readers to consider the punctuation of a text while they are reading. They should consider it as much as they do while writing. |
| | • If comprehension has broken down, make sure readers know to go back and check for missed punctuation marks. Punctuation embedded deep within quotes or sentences is often missed. Sometimes readers will liken the end of a line with the end of a sentence regardless of whether there is an end mark and whether it makes sense to end the sentence there. Sometimes a simple solution is to offer the reader a bookmark or a strip of paper to follow along down the page. |

What can family members/ caregivers do?	• Listen to your child read aloud. If he is sometimes ignoring punctuation marks, discuss their use and importance.
	• Encourage your child to read like a writer and write like a reader.
	• If your child is confused about what he is reading, remember to double-check for understanding and use of punctuation marks.

Dear family members and caregivers,

We have been talking about punctuation in reading this week. Yes, reading! You may think that punctuation lessons belong in writing, but we must remember that these marks tell the reader something about *how* the text should be read.

In an attempt to read quickly, some children skip punctuation marks. This is a dangerous mistake. Readers who do not use punctuation marks correctly are likely to lack understanding.

You can help by reminding your reader that

- A period is a signal to stop. The stop should be only long enough to take a breath, if necessary.

- A comma is a signal to make a quick pause. The pause for a comma is shorter than the pause for a period.

- An exclamation mark (!) signals excitement or urgency and should be read with expression.

- A sentence ending with a question mark should be read in the same way we ask a question. Our voices typically rise at the end of a question.

- A colon (:) signals the reader to stop and pause.

Listen to your reader often and take note of their use of punctuation.

Thank you for helping us grow as readers.

LESSON

Intonation, Voice, and Dialect

Miscue: The girl who sang all the high notes was a sŏprano.

What do you hear or see?

While reading with a boy in fifth grade, you notice him pronouncing words differently than you are accustomed to. You wonder if he is mispronouncing the words or is using a dialect you are not familiar with. Will saying these words differently affect his comprehension?

Why does it matter?

Intonation and dialect are important to constructing meaning. When we read a text, we often "hear" the characters speaking in a regional dialect that sounds different from our own. Sometimes the text is written in dialect, making this easier for the reader. Other times, we are left to pull from our own prior knowledge to construct the voices of characters. More important, intonation and dialect are vital in constructing meaning as we read aloud or when someone reads to us. When reading *Voices of the Alamo* by Sherry Garland (2000), the reader hears the story from sixteen different characters who bring sixteen unique voices and dialects to the story. When reading the carefully crafted language of the text aloud, it is almost impossible not to project the voices of the characters.

As teachers, we try to model standard English in our classrooms. Often, when we hear a child pronounce a word differently we immediately believe it is a mistake on the child's part. Clark will never forget the experience of moving from Iowa to Alabama when he was just nine years old. Truly a stranger in a strange land, his new life demanded many accommodations. One accommodation he failed to make was how to pronounce the word *grease*. In his fourth grade classroom he was asked to identify the sound of the letter /s/ in the word *grease*. He wrote in his workbook that the /s/ made an /s/ sound. When his answer was marked incorrect, he precociously thought his new teacher had made a mistake. "No, sweetheart," the new teacher tenderly explained, "The /s/ makes the same sound as the letter /z/ in the word *grease*."

Enlightened teachers are aware of the great impact a child's dialect has on all three of the cueing systems—semantic, syntactic, and phonological. Before correcting a child's seemingly mispronounced word, make sure it is truly a mispronunciation and not a product of dialect. Had Clark's teacher been more enlightened regarding to how people around our country (and our world for that matter) speak, she would have recognized *her* mistake!

What do you do?

Regardless of the age of the children you work with or the socioeconomic status of your students, hopefully yours is a classroom with a great sense of belonging and community, a place where everyone's ideas and values are viewed with merit. If this is the case, it goes without saying that the way each child speaks is valued. Some classrooms abound with diversity whereas others are islands of sameness. Wherever your classroom lies on the continuum of diversity, encourage your students to listen carefully to and celebrate the various accents and dialects in your classroom. Celebrate the beauty of dialect.

What can the reader do independently and collaboratively?

Students may want to make lists of varying pronunciations for words that they hear within the classroom and around the school building. The second grader from Jamaica is going to pronounce the word *man* quite differently from the fifth grade student who is visiting the United States from London, England.

Students may also want to make an oral or visual dictionary of different accents and dialects. Voices from around the school could be tape-recorded, and information about the speaker's region or country of origin could be recorded. Photographs could accompany the speakers' biographical information. Be sure to include both children and adults.

What can family members/ caregivers do?

The families of our children need to realize and understand the importance of the younger generation being more comfortable with various groups of people. Our world is becoming increasingly more diverse. This diversity is being reflected in the faces of the children we teach in our classrooms. Only when we make an attempt to understand one another better will we ever begin to get along.

Dear family members and caregivers,

We have been talking about the importance of intonation and dialect in our reading this week.

Intonation is the tone in which we read. As adults, we recognize that the words spoken by the frustrated bear who has been swindled out of his honey will sound different from the grandmother who is sharing her fondest memories with her grandchildren. The way we speak the words when we read them helps us understand the characters better. When children are young, we share this when we read aloud to them. As they grow older, they continue to hear this intonation as they read silently to themselves.

Although fun to talk about, dialect can be a challenge for both adults and children to read aloud, because we each possess a dialect that is unique. Sometimes, words that are written to reflect a specific dialect even look different on the page. When sharing books with your reader, do not be afraid to attempt the dialects of the characters. Have fun with dialects and celebrate our differences. Talk about people you know who hail from other parts of the country or world.

Thank you for helping us grow as readers.

Long Pauses

Miscue: The boy ρ/16 sec. sauntered out of the classroom.

What do you hear or see?

While listening to a student read, you notice that she pauses between words and phrases. Sometimes the pauses seem painfully long; at other times they are relatively brief. When she gets to the end of a line of text, she seems to search frantically for the beginning of the next line. Shouldn't she at least have a smooth return sweep by second grade?

Why does it matter?

Pauses, especially those that occur within phrases, almost certainly affect understanding. These pauses are symptomatic of several possible issues.

What do you do?

First, you must try to determine the root of the problem. We have had some success when we gently inquire about possible causes for the long pause. Listening to what children can tell us about how they process print is almost always beneficial.

If the reader is young or struggles with text, it is possible that she has a problem tracking print. In such cases, sweeping the finger below the text might solve part of the problem. Children who point to the text in a staccato, word-by-word manner will read in like manner and must be shown how to glide their fingers just below the printed word. The return sweep is also the cause of many long pauses while the reader's eyes search for the next line of text. In these cases, a piece of paper or card that masks the text, uncovering it line by line, may help to train the eye. We have also observed long pauses that are caused by growing fingers that simply get in the way, thus indicating a reader who is tracking print long past the need to do so. In these cases, sweeping the fingers below the text has become a bad habit. We then prompt the reader to track the print only with his or her eye.

Long pauses might also be noted because the reader is using word-solving strategies that take time. If the student is pausing at words that are presumed difficult, that is relatively easy for you to correct. However, when students pause before words that are seemingly simple, it would behoove you to look a few words down the line to analyze the text read *after* the pause, even if the text is read as written. Was there a difficult word three words later? Because the human eye works more quickly than we process and speak, it is possible that the student's eye was reading down the line and encountered a problematic word. Her mind set to work solving this word, thus creating the pause prior to a seemingly simple word. In this case, work with multisyllabic words might be appropriate. These students can also benefit from cloze experiences in which we coach readers to monitor their reading closely enough to predict difficult words. Children have engaged in such activities for years, but often have no idea how this technique can actually help them as readers.

Pauses can also indicate that students have an underdeveloped concept of prosody and phrasing. Teachers model both constantly but rarely discuss either with their students. In such cases is it appropriate to discuss with children the attributes of reading that "sounds good." An anchor chart that describes what fluent reading sounds like will support students who are attempting to offer feedback to classmates about their reading.

What can the reader do independently and collaboratively?

- Encourage the student to read and record appropriate texts. After listening to the playback and reflecting on the pauses in the reading, have the student record subsequent readings until he is satisfied with what he hears.
- Provide ample opportunities for the student to practice reading in a supportive, collaborative setting. Buddy reading followed by appropriate responses can support readers who are attempting to eliminate long pauses from their reading.
- A reader's theater or poetry reading center will provide authentic opportunities for students to collaborate and practice reading. Prosody and phrasing are more obvious in these forms of reading, thus supporting readers through potential long pauses.

What can family members/ caregivers do?

- Listen and provide appropriate, supportive feedback.
- Ask questions. When asked in the correct tone of voice, a simple, "Do you have any idea why you had to pause there?" will elicit an honest response. Do not barrage them with questions, but asking simple questions will provide family members and caregivers with the same beneficial information that it provides to teachers.
- Be sure that children have texts that are easy to read. We remind caregivers that it is always better to err on the side of too easy than too difficult.
- Model fluent reading by reading aloud to children at any age. If this is not possible, book and tape sets are available at almost all public libraries.

Meaning Change Omissions

What do you hear or see?

While reading with a student, you begin to realize he is omitting words that consistently change the meaning of what is being read. A simple example would be the child omitting the word *egg* from the opening sentence of the Eric Carle classic *The Very Hungry Caterpillar* (1969): "In the light of the moon a little egg lay on a leaf." As we mention in the lesson about skipping lines, proficient readers do indeed skip words as they predict, check, and confirm as they read. Skipping the words *the, moon,* or *little* does not affect the meaning of the sentence. But, skipping the words *light, egg, lay,* or *leaf* certainly does. A more complex sentence comes from Eve Bunting's Caldecott Award-winning book, *Smoky Night* (1994b). Bunting begins the tale set during the riots of Los Angeles with, "Mama and I stand well back from our window, looking down. I'm holding Jasmine, my cat. We don't have our lights on though it's almost dark. People are rioting in the streets below." A reader omitting the word *lights* loses the detail of the two characters standing in the dark, observing the riots. Even more difficult and less familiar words such as *Jasmine*, the name of the cat, and *rioting* do not change the meaning of the passage when omitted.

Why does it matter?

Proficient readers read carefully and monitor their comprehension as they read. Proficient readers skip words that are easily predicted. Words such as *a, is, are, that,* and so forth, are often skipped because they are correctly predicted and confirmed by the reader and skipped over by their rapidly moving eye. However, from time to time words are omitted or skipped that are crucial to understanding what is being read.

What do you do?

Make readers of all ages and abilities aware of the importance of reading carefully. Explain to them that two types of words are often skipped: words we know and our eyes and brain recognize very quickly, and words we are unsure of and have not encountered before. Sometimes a word is skipped unintentionally, as in the example of *lights* from the passage highlighted earlier. Readers may be interested in knowing which words our brains skip over the most often.

Be careful not to become an advocate of slow, cumbersome, word-by-word reading. Reading in this manner is slow and tiresome, and greatly impedes comprehension as attention is shifted from overall meaning to the meaning of isolated words. Word-by-word reading also affects fluency and rate of reading. Rather, instill within your readers the importance of reading carefully and of being aware of important words they may be omitting. Provide strategies to use when encountering a challenging or unknown word (break the word down into known parts, sound it out, use words just before and just after it to help estimate the meaning, and so on).

What can the reader do independently and collaboratively?	Provide students with laminated pieces of text suitable for their reading ability. Have them circle with a green water-based pen the words they believe could be omitted that *do not* change the meaning of the piece. Using a red pen, have them circle the words that *do* change the meaning of the piece when omitted. Pieces of text can be found in in children's literature, periodicals, textbooks, and so forth.
What can family members/ caregivers do?	Send the laminated passages and colored pens home in plastic bags and let the children see if their parents can determine which words can and cannot be omitted from the passages.

Meaning Change Omission Exercise

Mama and I stand well back from our window, looking down. I'm holding Jasmine, my cat. We don't have our lights on though it's almost dark. People are rioting in the streets below.

Mama explains about rioting, "It can happen when people get angry. They want to smash and destroy. They don't care anymore what's right and what's wrong."

Below us they are smashing everything. Windows, cars, streetlights.

(From Eve Bunting's *Smoky Night,* 1994b)

In the light of the moon a little egg lay on a leaf. One Sunday morning the warm sun came up and—pop!—out of the egg came a tiny and very hungry caterpillar.

(From Eric Carle's *The Very Hungry Caterpillar,* 1969)

Multisyllabic Words

hydro-
hy-

cata-
cat-

atmos-
at-

Miscue: The machine had a hydraulic lift that catapulted the missile into the atmosphere.

What do you hear or see?

While reading with a small group, you notice that two readers struggle with multisyllabic words. The miscues sometimes affect the meaning and impede comprehension. One reader omits all multisyllabic words whereas the other reader only omits them occasionally.

Why does it matter?

As readers become more proficient and competent, they encounter lengthier text, which is often composed of numerous multisyllabic words. It has been suggested that readers plateau in or around third grade as multisyllabic words become more prevalent in their reading. Even proficient readers need help knowing how to decode and thus arrive at the meanings of multisyllabic words. Decoding alone is not enough. Knowing the meanings of multisyllabic words is important to understanding the text. These readers need to develop strategies to figure out words they view as being too lengthy or too hard to read.

What do you do?

Choose a passage with numerous multisyllabic words. Have a conversation with the child about the importance of these words. Multisyllabic words can be nouns, common or proper, specifically telling us about which person, place, or thing we are reading. Other times they are verbs conveying a strong action. Still other times they are adverbs, deftly showing the reader how an action is performed. Sometimes they are adjectives, helping us paint a more vivid picture of what we are reading. Regardless of their part of speech, multisyllabic words are important and need to be understood, not shunned, by readers. Think aloud for the student by demonstrating what strategies you use as you come across multisyllabic words:

- Encourage the reader to skip the word and go back to consider words that make sense.
- Ask the reader to look at the word to decide whether there are chunks he knows. Place your finger over the chunks and see if he can determine the meaning of the words. Model this word-solving strategy during several minilessons.
- The word may not be in the child's vocabulary, and he may not be familiar with the word and its meaning. If the word is invaluable to understanding the text, it may be worth the investment of time to consult the dictionary.

- Demonstrate the prevalence of multisyllabic words during a shared reading by underlining or highlighting multisyllabic words in the text.
- Come back to these marked words at convenient stopping points. Create a T chart or similar graphic organizer and record the possible meanings of the words and check your predictions in a dictionary.

What can the reader do independently and collaboratively?	• After the shared reading experience, have readers mark multisyllabic words during independent reading. These words can be discussed during individual reading conferences and small group reading discussions.
	• Read! An adult friend of ours has a particularly strong vocabulary. One evening at dinner we remarked about her extensive word knowledge and inquired as to what her secret was. She stated simply that she reads voraciously. She reads with a dictionary at arm's length and looks up new words as she comes across them, all the time adding them to her already vast vocabulary. The same practice rings true for young readers as well.
	• Do not be leery of multisyllabic words. Daily, we encourage children to solve difficult math problems. We tell them to not be afraid and to begin dissecting the problem by beginning with the parts they know. The same strategy should be utilized when coming across a lengthy, intimidating multisyllabic word. Often daunting to readers, we should encourage them to look for chunks they know and give their best attempt at making sense of the word. Just like in math, sometimes the unknown is not as intimidating after it is better understood.
What can family members/ caregivers do?	Even if you believe your child can read, continue to listen to him read. Often, parents listen less and less to their children read as they become more able to read independently. Be wary of this trap. Just because a child can read does not mean they have nothing left to learn about how to read. Listening to them read aloud, even just once in a while, will provide you with a window into what your reader may need help with.

Nonlinear Text in Fiction and Nonfiction

What do you hear or see?

After reading with a student who you know reads well above grade level, you notice that she can read each of the words on the page, but does not possess a full understanding of what she just read. You are concerned about her inability to follow the text of the book she has chosen. You are both concerned over the frustration she experienced while reading a book she is very much interested in. After considering what the interferences to comprehension might be, you conclude that it is her unfamiliarity with nonlinear text that is impeding her comprehension.

Why does it matter?

Nonlinear text is akin to nonlinear plot. As children's book publishing becomes more advanced and more creative in our ever-growing technological age, teachers, parents, and, most important, children, are seeing more text presented in a nonlinear fashion. We are seeing the directionality of print blossom from the traditional left-to-right format to unique, creative formats that encompass every style of print you can imagine.

Children are most familiar with text that is presented to them in a linear format. A linear format is simply text presented in a line-by-line fashion. Linear text offers no surprises and is presented in a very familiar, upfront manner. It is read from left to right, down the page.

Nonlinear text is the direct opposite of linear text. Nonlinear text can be described as text that is presented in any format other than line-by-line. Authors, illustrators, editors, and publishers arrange text on a page to add to the book's meaning, utility, and aesthetic effect. Nonlinear text can come in the form of columns, wavy lines, spirals, borders, and the like. With the technological means now available, text can be laid out in a myriad of ways.

What do you do?

Teachers need to help their children unlock the mystery of nonlinear text. Once cost prohibitive and rarely seen, nonlinear text is becoming much more common across the genres of children's literature. When children lose the support of reading text presented in a familiar left-to-right format, they must replace it with another strategy. To construct meaning, students must understand how to adjust their eyes, their tracking, and their thinking to unknown styles of print direction. Readers need to know how to maneuver nonlinear text. Demonstrate to them what strategies readers use while dealing with nonlinear text. Strategies include:

- Knowing that nonlinear text can be challenging to follow and understand
- Knowing that books with nonlinear text will probably need to be read more than once. Indeed, they may need to be read several times to construct thorough meaning.
- Knowing that nonlinear text is much like a road map through the book. You cannot follow all the roads at once. You have to choose a road and follow it to the end. Then you can come back and follow another road. After you are familiar with all the nonlinear roads of the book, then you can jump on and off any road you wish.
- Choose which of the nonlinear paths of text you want to follow through the book the first time you read it and which paths you will follow on subsequent readings of the book.

Byrd Baylor makes use of nonlinear text in each of her books. Look for the classic *I'm in Charge of Celebrations* (1986) and *The Way to Start a Day* (1978), as well as *The Table Where Rich People Sit* (1998). Using Baylor's books, you can show children the columnar style in which the text is presented. Readers will most likely be unfamiliar with seeing just one or two words per line and will need practice reading the columnar format.

The classic nonfiction series, *The Magic School Bus* from Joanna Cole and Bruce Degen, contains nonlinear text. A favorite of students and teachers alike, these books are readily available and cover a wide range of science topics. Used in a minilesson, these books are examples of how to follow and read nonlinear text. Readers' comprehension will improve when they come to realize that there are many layers of text to read and understand. More important, they will understand more of the content when they know that they can skip some of the text and go back and reread it during a second, third, or fourth visit through the book. Cole and Degen's more recent, larger books contain nonlinear text as well. Look for *Mrs. Frizzle's Adventures: Medieval Castle* (2003) and *Mrs. Frizzle's Adventures: Imperial China* (2005).

Poetry abounds with nonlinear text. An intricate example of nonlinear text is found in Warren Hanson's *The Next Place* (1997). An inspiring poem celebrating life and what lies beyond our definition of it, each page presents the reader with challenging nonlinear text. Text is shown in short, wavy sentences; arching semicircles; even a sweeping star burst. Amazingly, even the bibliographic information at the beginning of the book is presented in a nonlinear format. Clark can remember the first time he came across this heart-warming book. Even reading it to himself, he had to go back and reread several of the pages before becoming familiar with the directionality of the print. Before reading it aloud for the first time, he had to practice many times to ward off confusing mistakes.

Ruth Wells' and Yoshi's alphabet book about Japanese culture, *A to Zen: A Book of Japanese Culture* (1992), can be used to show established readers of all ages that not all print is read left to right. Appropriately, the book opens from the right side or what English reading students would call the "back." The text is read from the right to the left. We would recommend sharing this book only with children who are firmly established in their concepts of print (Clay, 1994). To show this book to burgeoning readers might confuse them.

What can the reader do independently and collaboratively?

Readers of all ages need not be scared or intimidated by nonlinear text. Once they are introduced to the text and understand strategies for dealing with it, they are bound to come across it in other books they read. They could be encouraged to keep a list of books with nonlinear text they have read. Maybe there are books they have wanted to read, but did not because of the fact they were intimidated by the nonlinear text they held. Encourage them to return to those once passed-over books and enjoy them with confidence.

What can family members/ caregivers do?

Bring parents up to date on the latest in children's book publishing. Host a meeting in your classroom or meet at a local bookstore to hear about the latest and greatest in children's books. More than likely, you will come across nonlinear text in one format or another. Booksellers are often happy to speak to small groups about particular genres of literature. If you are lucky, they may even provide discounts or coupons to use toward your purchases!

Nonlinear Plots

What do you hear or see?

During a conference with a reader, you notice she has chosen a book you know contains a nonlinear plot. You are concerned over her lack of comprehension and feel it is the result of this unfamiliar story structure.

Why does it matter?

Following the basic plot of a story is a crucial component to comprehension. Without understanding the basic plot, there is no way readers can go on to understand more complicated aspects of what they are reading. Most often, a young reader or an inexperienced reader will stumble across a book with a nonlinear plot. More likely than not, this unfamiliar plot structure will strike them as odd and will become a barrier to further comprehension.

What do you do?

A simple minilesson with an individual reader, a small group, or possibly the entire class will help readers understand how to follow a nonlinear plot. You might begin the conversation discussing the word *linear* and how the word *line* is the root word. Even young children will realize a line is straight. Hopefully, you can aid the readers in making the connection between a straight line and a straight plot or one that consists of a clear beginning, middle, and end. Of course, if that is a straight plot, a nonlinear plot must follow anything but a straight path. Easily explained, a nonlinear plot flashes back and forth between the past, the present, and sometimes the future.

After this minilesson, examples of nonlinear plots could be shared. Preferably, you should begin with an example that is very straightforward, and then progress to examples that are more complicated. David Wiesner's 2002 Caldecott Award-winning book, *The Three Pigs* (2001), takes a story with a linear plot children are familiar with and gives it a very nonlinear twist. Beginning traditionally, the three pigs suddenly leave the pages of the plot to escape the big bad wolf. Their escape is brought to the forefront of the reader by a distinct change in illustrative style. They leap from the imaginary land of the traditional tale into a very realistically portrayed authentic world. (See lesson entitled Using Illustration to Aid Comprehension of a Nonlinear Plot.) While on the lam from their fantasy world, the pigs encounter and interact with other characters from similar nursery tales.

Louis Sachar's book, *Holes* (1984), winner of the 1999 Newbery Medal, follows a nonlinear plot. The book unfolds as much in the past as it does the present. Sachar uses chapter breaks to aid the reader in knowing when twists in the plot occur. Often, readers do not fully understand the author's intention until they are several chapters into the book and have had the guidance of a supportive teacher.

What can the reader do independently and collaboratively?

Readers need to be aware that sometimes authors utilize a nonlinear plot formation. They need to understand that not all plots are as straightforward as others. Readers may want to keep a list of hints or clues the author may use to help them realize a twist in the plot is about to occur. This list could be kept in a reading journal or posted for the entire class to view.

What can family members/ caregivers do?

Family members and caregivers alike need to be aware of nonlinear plots in children's literature. They need to understand that if their child is having difficulty following the plot of a story, that it may very well be because of a nonlinear plot. They need to know that it is perfectly acceptable to skim ahead a few lines, paragraphs, pages, or chapters to understand the plot better themselves. In this way, they will be able to support the needs of the reader.

Dear family members and caregivers,

Have you ever read a book that contained flashbacks or flash forwards and you sometimes felt lost inside the story? This week we have been talking about books with nonlinear plots. Books with nonlinear plots do not usually flow in a straight line from a simple beginning to a specific end. They tend to take side trips into the past or future and meander along multiple story lines.

This week we have talked about ways to recognize nonlinear plots and what to do when we encounter one. It is important to recognize a flashback or flash forward. We have noticed that these are sometimes written in differing type styles or are italicized. At other times these flashbacks or flash forwards are identifiable because they are contained within their own chapters.

When sharing books with your reader,

- Stop when you notice a flashback or flash forward. Talk about how you were able to recognize it.

- Talk often about how the flashbacks or flash forwards affect the story. Think about why they are important. Be patient. Keep in mind that many nonlinear plots do not become clear until the end of the book.

Thank you for helping us grow as readers.

Onomatopoeia

What do you hear or see?

A student rushes back from the library with a new book and proclaims it the best book he has ever read. He asks if he may read it aloud to the class. You ask that he practice reading it aloud at home that evening and make a note on the next day's schedule that he will read the book during share time.

The next day he enthusiastically positions himself before his classmates and begins to read *Shhh!* by Jeanne Willis (2004). You are impressed. He is reading beautifully with a great deal of expression. It is exactly the way you would expect someone to read "the best book" he has ever read to his friends.

Why does it matter?

Onomatopoeia is the formation of a word from a sound. It is important for children to know how to read these words correctly because they require the correct expression. Although onomatopoeia can occasionally be a decoding problem for some children, more often than not, it is an expression issue.

What do you do?

As with other literary devices, find examples of onomatopoeia in age-appropriate texts. Explain to the children that just as authors work hard to help us visualize what we read, they often work just as hard to help us hear what they want for us to hear. At times, they even include sound effects. Go on to explain that sometimes these sound effects are written in all capital letters followed by an exclamation point. We tell children that words written in all capital or oversized letters are the equivalent of yelling on paper, especially if the word is followed by an exclamation mark. If the word in the text is "CRASH!" then it should be read in such a way that the audience knows there was a loud sound.

At other times, the sound effect will be italicized. This indicates that the author wants for us to hear a softer, more gentle sound inside of our heads. If the text says, "The long grass went *swish-swash, swish-swash*," the audience would expect a soothing, quiet sound that reminds them of grass blowing in a gentle breeze. In the book *Shhh!*, the noise that the shrew is trying is written in big, dark letters of various fonts. When the shrew speaks, the letters are italicized and printed in normal font size and style.

What can the reader do independently and collaboratively?

- Look for examples of onomatopoeia in text. Have readers add these words to a class list of "sound" words. This is helpful when children want to use sound effects in their writing.

- Practice reading stories and poems that contain onomatopoeia with a buddy or small group. It does affect the way reading should sound. Reading the words in such a way that the mood of the piece is maintained is one element of fluency and does affect comprehension.

- Remind children to experiment with onomatopoeia in their writing.

Point of View

Text: I wish the sun would stop shining. I wish the temperature would go below freezing. I really like the way the kids put the three large snowballs together. They were just the right size. I even like how they used coal and a carrot to make my face.

In the retelling, it becomes obvious 6the reader does not realize the story was written from the point of view of a snowman.

What do you hear or see?

You have just listened to a student in your room read a passage from a self-selected text. You note in your anecdotal records that she read with intonation, expression, and fluency, and made no meaning-changing miscues. Feeling satisfied with the interaction and confident the reader can continue without your presence, you are poised to move along to your next conferee. Almost as an afterthought, you ask the reader: "Who was telling what you just read?" Your suspicions prove right when the reader looks at you with a blank face. Obviously, she has no idea from whose point of view the text has been written.

Why does it matter?

Understanding point of view is crucial to comprehending what is read. Changes in points of view make all the difference in the world to the meaning of the writing. Readers often miss this important aspect of reading. Young, egocentric children assume that the point of view is always obvious or, more alarming, not important to consider at all.

What do you do?

- Read a traditional version of *The Three Little Pigs*. Discuss from whose point of view the traditional tale is told. Follow the traditional version with *The True Story of the Three Pigs* by Scieszka and Smith (1998), and Wiesner's Caldecott Award-winning, postmodern adaptation *The Three Pigs* (2001). Help the reader recognize the very different viewpoints of these three books. Of course, the traditional version is told from the point of view of the pigs. Scieszka and Smith's version is told from the point of view of the wolf and offers a very different tale than you might suspect. Wiesner's foray into the tale of the three pigs shows a pig's-eye perspective of what could happen in a fantasy gone awry.

- Shel Silverstein offers a poem in his timeless anthology of poetry, *Where the Sidewalk Ends* (1974), aptly entitled, "Point of View" (98). Consisting of three short stanzas, the poem adeptly looks at the family dinner ritual from the dinner's point of view. After a shared reading of this poem, young readers are sure never to look at food the same way again.

- Encourage readers to tackle differing points of view in their writing. Discuss other authors' writing during writing and reading workshop. How would Roald Dahl's timeless treasure *Willy Wonka and the Chocolate Factory* (1998) have been different if told from the point of view of an Oompa-Loompa? What a different feel Natalie Babbitt's *Tuck Everlasting* (1975) would have if told from the eyes of the sinister man in the yellow suit!

What can the reader do independently and collaboratively?

Remind readers to be conscious of points of view, not only in their reading and writing, but in their everyday lives as well. Point out differing views as they arise in your classroom community. Older readers might enjoy reading the various points of view offered on the editorial page of your local newspaper.

Dear family members and caregivers,

There truly are two sides to every story. This week we have been talking about point of view in our reading. Have you ever considered the story of the three pigs told from the wolf's point of view? Could it be that the wolf was actually an innocent victim of the three pigs?

Point of view is a key element of stories. It can truly change how you feel about a character or a story. Sometimes the books young children choose to read are not told from the point of view that you might expect. This is particularly troublesome when the stories are told in the first person. If the character in a book refers to him or herself as "I," children will often be confused about who is actually telling the story.

When discussing a book with an older reader, point of view flavors how we understand the book. Just as in the real world of everyday life, characters have unique personalities and experiences that must be considered when thinking about their actions and how they relate to the story.

You can help your reader consider point of view by

- Constantly reminding him or her to consider other points of view
- Reading appropriate editorials in newspapers or magazines and discussing the possible feelings and points of view of the writers
- Talking about point of view after watching movies or television programs together.

Our favorite books for discussing point of view include:

- *Atlantic* by G. Brian Karas (2002)
- *Something to Tell the Grandcows* by Eileen Spinelli (2004)
- *Water Dance* by Thomas Locker (1997)
- *Our Tree Named Steve* by Alan Zweibel (2005)
- *I, Crocodile* by Fred Marcellino (1999)
- *Project Mulberry* by Linda Sue Park (2005)
- *Two Bad Ants* by Chris Van Allsburg (1988)

Thank you for helping us grow as readers.

Prior Knowledge

What do you hear or see?

As proficient readers, we realize the importance of prior knowledge. Prior knowledge, or schema, is what you already know about a topic. The more prior knowledge you bring to what you are reading, the easier it will be to understand. Comprehension breaks down when very little prior knowledge exists about the subject being read. Often, children of all ages are assigned or given reading about topics in which they possess very little prior knowledge. Thus, they begin reading the piece at a deficit and seldom recover.

Why does it matter?

Prior knowledge is helpful in understanding what you are reading. As proficient readers ourselves, we have each encountered text with subjects about which we had little prior experience. Anyone who is not a trained accountant and has tried to read and comprehend the US tax code will attest to the fact that prior knowledge is key to understanding. We can easily attest to the difficulty we had in comprehending this text until a sufficient amount of prior knowledge was constructed. Sometimes readers have limited prior knowledge that is not sufficient for deep understanding. It is important that we not mistake enthusiasm for prior knowledge. However, desire and interest can motivate a reader to forge ahead through difficult text. Once, when studying bodily systems, a student became fascinated with the circulatory system. Determined to become the world's youngest cardiologist, he rushed to the library and borrowed two very difficult pieces of nonfiction. Although he struggled through parts of the weighty text, he satisfied his desire to know more about the human heart and the oxygenation of blood.

What do you do?

Remind the children that prior knowledge is what you know about a topic before you begin reading. The information in your schema is invaluable to comprehension.

Before you begin reading a new book, think about what you already know about it. Model this with your students, and take the time to wonder about the text aloud. Record your wonderings for later reflection.

Discuss what to do when you lack sufficient knowledge to understand a text. Children must be given strategies to build their own prior knowledge during multiple minilessons. To do this effectively, you must be keenly aware of the interests of your students. We have observed that most children share a fascination with the *Titanic*. Most children walk straight to Robert D. Ballard's *Exploring the Titanic* (1988). Although a marvelous book, for a child who has no schema for the story, it is probably not a wise choice. Fortunately, there have been a multitude of texts written about the tragedy that run the gamut of readability and detail. We show the students several of these books and model how we would read the shortest, simplest book first. We follow this lesson with subsequent readings of increasing difficulty and detail. In the end, when sufficient prior knowledge has been established, we turn to Ballard's book. In this way we model how we scaffold ourselves into learning about new things.

What can the reader do independently and collaboratively?	• Maintain a log of topics of interest.
	• Become an expert on topics of personal interest. Providing there is ample text, this allows children to build deep prior knowledge.
	• Participate in nonfiction book clubs and research groups.

Proper Nouns

What do you hear or see?

While administering a QRI, you note the reader often pauses for extended amounts of time. They also omit or mispronounce words often. Slowly, you begin to realize the pauses, the omissions, and the mispronunciations occur when a proper noun is encountered. You further observe and make note that the reader sometimes substitutes a more familiar name for a more challenging one (i.e., Lewis for Lopez or Carl for Carlos). Though some of the substitutions may not alter the meaning of the piece being read, omissions most probably do. How do you know who went to the birthday party if you skip over Maria's name entirely?

Why does it matter?

Like multisyllabic words, proper nouns are important facets of any piece of writing. They tell the reader about which people, places, and things they are reading. Proficient readers suspect that the very names of people and places referred to in a piece of writing are always key elements to understanding the writing. Readers who are not concerned with proper nouns are sometimes more concerned with accuracy than they are the actual meaning of the text. Remember, accuracy without comprehension does not result in meaningful reading.

What do you do?

Explain to the reader that

- Sometimes pronouncing the names of geographical locations and people's names is difficult for adults, too.
- Oftentimes it is impossible to decode the correct pronunciation. Think about the city names Des Moines, Cheyenne, and San Jose. You can't begin to sound them out correctly. The same is true for people's names like Mutay, Beate, and Xing. Again, you can't begin to sound them out.
- Remember, reading is about understanding the words on the page; not about pronouncing all of the words correctly.
- Remind children that their prior knowledge is always useful when considering proper nouns.
- Time spent trying to sound out proper nouns is a waste of the child's reading energy. Other elements of the story need their attention.
- Believe it or not, sometimes you don't even have to pronounce a person's name or the name of a city correctly to fully understand what it is you are reading.
- Think about people you could ask to help you with the challenging proper noun. Is there a geography expert in the class? Has someone else in the class read the same book before? How did they rise to the challenge of negating the proper nouns?

What can the reader do independently and collaboratively?

- Brainstorm a list of favorite book characters. Discuss how, for instance, E. B. White's classic, *Charlotte's Web,* is just as meaningul if the pig's name is Wilbur or Eugene.
- Look at the work of Dr. Seuss and notice how not knowing how to pronounce the character's names does not interfere at all with comprehending the text.
- Use an abbreviation for a person's difficult name or for a challenging place name.

Dear family members and caregivers,

We have been talking about proper nouns during our reading workshop. Please take time to discuss interesting names of family members and friends with your reader. It seems as if almost every family has more than their fair share of interesting names. Remember to discuss geographical place names as you travel, listen to or watch the news, and as you read. Consider purchasing an atlas or a globe, as children are fascinated by different places on our planet.

You may also want to encourage your reader to read nonfiction. Biographies and autobiographies are full of interesting proper nouns. The same can be said for any historical piece. Make sure your home is full of weekly periodicals and newspapers.

Thank you for helping us grow as readers.

Questioning

What do you hear or see?

During reading workshop, a few kids continually "shop" for books. Every time you glance up, they seem to be milling around the book baskets, exchanging one book for another. You are confident in their abilities to read the text; however, you realize that they are not engaging with the text. As you browse through their reading journals you observe that their responses to their reading are superficial retellings. You decide to model your use of questioning as a comprehension and engagement strategy.

Why does it matter?

Valuing the questions generated by the reader is invaluable to helping him grow as a reader. Questions we have about characters and plot while we read prompt us to keep reading the book. We have all refused to put a book down for the night until we *know* whether the heroine of the book finds her way home. The questions we have keep the pages turning.

Every bit of sensory information conveys meaning and elicits questions. The interesting texture of the cover of Ed Young's *Beyond the Great Mountain: A Visual Poem about China* (2005) evokes questions immediately. When we first saw this book we ran our hands over the paper again and again, questioning whether the cover was actually made of rice paper or made to look that way. This question begged us to open the book, where the end papers only prompted us to ask more questions. Before we knew it, we had questioned the entire book, and spent 10 minutes in the bookstore discussing possible answers to our questions. Reader-generated questions reach beyond the expected. When children attempt to clarify their thinking and answer their own questions, the results are powerful. Children are not only able to tell us the answers to their questions, but are also able to tell us *how* they arrived at those answers. In our experience, children tend to view questions as things only the teacher can ask. We have modeled questioning for students who were literally afraid to pose questions and would only dare do so after much teacher modeling and encouragement.

What do you do?

We recommend that you attempt to model this strategy as a shared read-aloud, in which all members of the classroom community participate in the questioning. We have found that it works best if the students have already had some practice making connections.

First, find intriguing books to question with your students. Not every book lends itself to deep questioning. Sarah Stewart has several titles—*The Money Tree* (1991), *The Friend* (2004), and *The Gardener* (1997)—that we have used with amazing results. We question all three of these texts as part of an author study. Not surprisingly, the children make text-to-text connections that lead to big questions about themes and the author's purpose.

We introduce questioning with an anchor chart that simply reminds the kids that good readers ask questions before they read, while they read, and after they read. We then explain that we are going to use every single inch of the book being read as we question. We inform the children that they will be asking the questions they wonder about out loud so we can record them on sticky notes. And so the lesson begins. We read the title, examine the front and back cover, and ask questions that pop into our minds about that information. We then look at the end papers, dedication, and author's note (if there is one), and ask questions we have about that information. We are often amazed by the number of powerful questions that emerge before we read a single word of the actual book. We then continue this process as we read through the text. You and your students must set your own parameters for the lesson. Will you consider every question asked by every student? Will you consider only one question from everyone? Will you stop at the end of every page to share and record questions or will you stop in strategically chosen places to do it? We have tried all these strategies and have found them all to be effective. You and your students know which framework best suits your situation.

We do actually record the questions on individual sticky notes during our initial lessons. We stick the notes to the pages that prompted the questions. We believe this is important because we want kids to know that good readers answer their own questions as well. Yes, this takes time. It is not uncommon for us to spend three or four days questioning a book. That may seem like a long time, but we haven't had a kid complain yet!

After we have read the book and recorded our questions, we set to work answering them. We encourage the kids to tell us about their thinking and remind them to tell the group how they arrive at their answers. We sort the questions as they are answered into one of five categories: answer in the text, answer in my schema, answer made by inference, need for further research, and question cannot be answered.

What can the reader do independently and collaboratively?

- Use this same technique during independent reading by coding the text or recording questions in the student's reading journal or on sticky notes. The reader can clarify his understanding by answering the questions after reading and sorting them as described earlier.
- Small collaborative groups can question through a text in the same way that the large group does. This is an interesting way to approach a book club or literature circle.

Our favorite picture books that elicit deep questions include:

Feathers and Fools by Mem Fox (1989)
Cecil's Story by George Ella Lyon (1991)
Fly Away Home by Eve Bunting (1991)
Allison by Allen Say (1991)
Amelia's Road by Linda Jacobs Altman (1999)
The Other Side by Jacqueline Woodson (2001)
Molly Bannaky by Alice McGill (1999)
Letting Swift River Go by Jane Yolen (1992a)
Roanoke, The Lost Colony by Jane Yolen (2003)
New Hope by Henri Sorenesen (1995)
The Man Who Walked Between the Towers by Mordicai Gerstein (2003)
The Big Box by Toni and Slade Morrison (1999)
Red Legs by Ted Lewin (2001)

How We Answer Questions

Questions answered with information from the text:	Questions answered with information from our schemas:	Questions that made us do some inferring:	Questions that need some research:	Questions we could not answer:

Realistic Fiction versus Fantasy

What do you hear or see?

It's nearing the end of the school year. You believe your fourth grade students have a firm grasp of the various genres of children's literature. You feel confident that most of the students in your class could explain that genres are groupings or categories of books that share common characteristics. You are pretty sure they realize that within genres, you can expect subgenres and that sometimes genres blend together to form hybrid genres.

You have tried to expose your students to quality children's literature from many different genres. Together, you have experienced all sorts of fiction. You have read books that are realistic fiction and others that are historical fiction. You have delved into the manipulative world of science fiction as well. You have read biographies and autobiographies about many different people from the past and the present. Together you have flown away to the land of fantasy and lost yourselves in an enchanted story. You have enjoyed the legends, fables, and tall tales associated with traditional literature and the rich lessons about life they evoke. You have experienced the joys and sorrows of collections of poetry. You have loved favorite picture books, and the nonfiction information books fly off the shelves of your classroom library. Their dog-eared pages barely hold together. With all this careful consideration of what your class reads and is read, you are still challenged by the notion that they still have a hard time distinguishing realistic fiction from fantasy.

Why does it matter?

Being able to discern realistic fiction from fantasy is very important if children are to understand the meaning of a book. Indeed, it can be argued that the lines between reality and fantasy are blurring in our very lives. What with the age of ever-improving technology we live in, you can never be sure if what you read, or see, is the truth. Does that snake really have two heads or has the picture been touched up with Photoshop? How much more realistic can the football players of the handheld video game be? Movies and television captivate young and old audiences alike with their ability to make fantasy seem as realistic as possible. With the technology of today and the impending technology of tomorrow, the impossible is truly becoming possible. We need to help our students be able to tell the difference between the two.

As adults, we all enjoy the momentary escape of falling into a book or movie of fantasy. We all need to suspend reality from time to time. Children are no different. They just need to know when they are doing it.

What do you do?

One thing you can do is to read Paul Fleischman's book, *Weslandia* (1999). After reading the tale about the boy who is an outcast and comes to create his own civilization, ask who thinks Wesley is a character from the genre of fantasy and who thinks he fits better with the genre of realistic fiction. (Surprisingly, with all of the book's fantastical elements, some children are bound to think the book could actually happen.) Create a T chart to organize their answers and thinking about Wesley. On one side of the T chart list the attributes of Wesley that seem very realistic; on the other side, list those that seem very unrealistic. Some of the realistic attributes of Wesley include his feelings of isolation and loneliness. His feeling of being an outcast and longing for acceptance are emotions children can readily identify with and consider very real. Wesley also has trouble interacting with his peers and has interests very different from theirs.

Some of Wesley's more fantastical attributes the children might mention are the magical wind that blows in from the west one night planting his land with seeds as magical as the beans that grew Jack's beanstalk. That the fruit his plants produce tastes like a combination of peach, strawberry, pumpkin, and flavors he had no name for is unusual. That he was able to weave cloth from his plant's fibers is unique. That he was able to create a new language system based on an 80-letter alphabet is highly unlikely.

It may take more than one class session to complete both sides of your T chart about Wesley. When both sides of the chart are completed, have the class consider which side makes a stronger case. Is Wesley more a real character or is he more of a character of the imagination? Hopefully, they will be able to see plainly that so much of what constitutes Wesley's character is make believe, and they will come to the conclusion that the book fits best into the category of fantasy.

What can the reader do independently and collaboratively?

Have the children of your class use the same T chart to consider the plausibility of other characters and books they are having a hard time placing in the category of realistic fiction or fantasy. Could the book *Holes* by Louis Sachar (1984) *really* happen? As much as we want to believe in Winnie and the Tuck's family struggle with eternal life, could the events of *Tuck Everlasting* (Babbitt, 1975) ever actually occur? The better children get at distinguishing between reality and fantasy, the better they will be at understanding the skill it takes an author and/or illustrator to create a fantasy world for us to believe in.

Dear family members and caregivers,

In recent days we have been talking about the differences between realistic fiction and fantasy. In the mind of a child it can be hard to tell the difference between these two kinds of books. With our world becoming more technologically advanced by the minute, this distinction is harder to distinguish. Movies, computer games, and television have blurred the lines between fantasy and reality. Even reality television programs are not based in reality. Remember that a story that can really happen is considered realistic fiction. If the book actually happened, it is then considered nonfiction. Obviously, books that are considered fantasy could never truly occur.

When sharing books with your reader,

- Discuss the aspects of the book that are believable and those that are not.

- Talk about what makes a book or character believable or not.

- Read books that are fiction as well as nonfiction to your reader. We tend to choose fiction more often than nonfiction. Excellent nonfiction text is available at all levels.

- Don't forget to remind him or her that much information on the Internet is subject to interpretation and may not be based on reality.

Thank you for helping us grow as readers.

Repetitions and Unnecessary Reruns

What do you hear or see?

While conducting a fluency check, you note that the reader repeats words and phrases, sometimes three or more times. He even repeated an entire line of text without batting an eye. To add to your confusion, there were no miscues.

Why does it matter?

Unnecessary reruns, especially those in which children reread entire lines of text, are an indication that the child is not self-monitoring. This reader is not actively engaged in the reading process and is not making meaning from the print as he reads. Because the ultimate goal of fluency is understanding, this miscue is troubling on several levels.

What do you do?

It is possible that children who repeat single words and short phrases are rereading to aid their own comprehension, but they may also be engaging in nothing more than a bad habit. Reread a fluency check aloud to the student, complete with the repeated words and/or phrases. You will often see smiles and hear giggles. We have encountered children who simply never realized they had a large number of reruns. Of course, anyone who has attempted to break a bad habit realizes that this is easier said than done. You might try

- Teaching children how to listen for fluent reading. Create an anchor chart to remind children how to give fluency feedback.
- Modeling fluent and nonfluent reading and asking the students to practice responding. Be sure that you model short reruns, as well as reruns of entire lines.
- Enlisting the help of a peer. Teach the students how to code reruns by placing a line under a word each time it is repeated. Have the buddy share the coded reruns. Allow the student to practice reading the text several times until the reruns no longer occur. Buddy reading with supportive coaching can help break the habit.

It is also possible that the child is not actually attending to the reading. We have encountered children who seemingly go on autopilot during fluency checks, thinking speed is the desired outcome.

- Fluent reading is not synonymous with fast reading. Remind children of this fact daily. Model all the elements of fluent reading when you read aloud.
- Ask children to do a quick retelling of what has been read. This will let you know if someone has zoned out during the reading. If the child cannot retell the passage, remind her that reading is thinking, and try it again.

Sometimes reruns are made when children make multiple attempts to decode unfamiliar words. In this case, the reruns are necessary for comprehension, but impede fluency. Reruns actually indicate a child who is self-monitoring. Thorough miscue analysis will inform your instructional decisions about such readers. These kids may need work in other areas (see multisyllabic words, names, and context clues) before you can shore up the reader's fluency.

What can the reader do independently and collaboratively?	• Practice with appropriate text. If the reader is to practice independently, the text must be at the reader's independent level. • The reader can read to a peer and request feedback. • Tape-record readings and reflect on her own fluency.
What can family members/ caregivers do?	• Listen and provide appropriate, supportive feedback. • Be sure that children have texts that are easy to read. We remind caregivers that it is always better to err on the side of too easy than too difficult. • Model fluent reading by reading aloud to children at any age. If this is not possible, book and tape sets are available at almost all public libraries.

Retelling/Summarizing

What do you hear or see?

Readers who have difficulty retelling or summarizing what they have just read generally react in one of two ways. They either cannot recall one fact about what they have read or they retell with painstaking detail, unable to summarize what they are reading. Maryann, Shelly, and Clark often see this situation arise during the retelling section of the QRI or similar reading assessments.

Why does it matter?

As teachers, we know that the ability to retell what has just been read is indicative of how well what was read is understood. Retelling, summarizing, putting what you have read into your own words—each of these like abilities signifies a student who is constructing meaning while she reads.

What do you do?

- Scaffold children into their own retellings by encouraging them to retell what has been read aloud to them during shared, guided, or read-aloud reading. In this instance, the challenge of actually reading has been surmounted and the reader is free to set her sights on retelling.
- Model the process of retelling with the whole class. After a picture book read-aloud of appropriate content and length for your age group, work with the class as they construct a retelling of the book.
- Further utilize the gradual release model as described by Harvey and Goudvis (2000) by having students do impromptu retellings after you read a picture book or a chapter or two from your daily read-aloud book. Remember, students should have a good idea of what constitutes a good retelling. Clark picked up from a colleague the idea of having students complete a retelling once each grading period. Books were chosen that were similar in length and genre so that each of the retellings could be compared and contrasted as the year progressed. The work of Patricia Polacco is well suited for this task. The retellings were housed in students' portfolios and were referred to during parent conferences. At the end of the year, it was refreshing to see how much the students' ability to retell had improved. A reproducible has been included for your use.

What can the reader do independently and collaboratively?

- Have readers complete a GIST (see reproducible) of what they have read. A GIST is simply a twenty-word retelling. Because the number of words is limited, word choice becomes paramount. Shelly has utilized GISTS in many ways throughout the years. Her favorite use of the GIST strategy is to have students write a GIST after each chapter book they read aloud together as a class. Clark uses the strategy with his second graders as well. The students complete GISTS at the end of a chapter book read-aloud. Each GISTS is discussed and an overall class favorite is selected to post in the classroom. The hanging GISTS serve as warm reminders of the books they have shared together.
- Have students complete a retelling of what they are reading independently.
- Consider how you could utilize retelling across the curriculum. Could students retell sections of what they have read in social studies or science? Could they retell the directions to solving a multistep math problem? Could they put events in chronological order? The uses of retellings are many.

What can family members/ caregivers do?

Send home copies of the GIST form and retelling blocks (see reproducible, page 116) for family members and caregivers to use while working with their children.

Retelling

Name: _____ Date: _____

Title of book: _____

Author and Illustrator: _____

Pages/Chapter told about: _____

_____

_____

_____

_____

_____

_____

_____

_____

_____

_____

_____

_____

GIST

_____ _____ _____ _____

_____ _____ _____ _____

_____ _____ _____ _____

_____ _____ _____ _____

_____ _____ _____ _____

Then . . .

Finally . . .

Then . . .

Then . . .

First . . .

Then . . . .

Setting

What do you hear or see?

During a retelling, you notice the third grader you are working with gives you multiple answers when you ask him the setting of the book. You know the book takes place in just one location and wonder why he thinks there are so many different settings in the book.

Why does it matter?

Authors use setting to help support the story about which they write. The setting must be carefully researched and portrayed accurately or the story is not believable. Children are often not able to generalize beyond the word-by-word or page-by-page settings an author and illustrator create in a picture book. That is the problem the student mentioned here is having. He has just read Christopher Myers's *Black Cat* (1999). When asked about the setting, instead of giving you the one-word answer you anticipate (in the *city*, in *Harlem*, *downtown*), he provides you with nearly another retelling of the book: "First the cat is near the subway. Then, the cat is on the roof of a building. Then, the cat is on the basketball court. Then, the cat is on the playground." Clearly, this student is not able to generalize beyond the pages he recalls and views the book—and the setting—as a whole.

What do you do?

Shelly has devised and used a simple diagram to help students become aware of the "bigger picture" of setting. The diagram is included at the end of this lesson and consists of concentric circles. Each circle provides a space to list the page-by-page settings children so often provide. Start with the first setting they offer and move outward from the center. Shelly has used this diagram with students of all ages and in groups of all sizes, ranging from a whole class to an individual.

When you reach the second-to-last outermost band, stop and discuss the setting of the book with your class, small group, or individual student. Your discussion may go something like this: "We have listed all these places where we think the book took place. And each of them is correct. Each ring is a place mentioned in the story. What I am wondering is where do they *all* take place? What do they all have in common?" This is the point at which students will begin to see the bigger picture of setting.

The same exercise could be done with a chapter book as well. Consider this paragraph from Phyllis Reynolds Naylor's book, *Shiloh* (1991, 12):

> We live high up in the hills above Friendly, but hardly anybody knows where
> that is. Friendly's near Sistersville, which is halfway between Wheeling and

Parkersburg. Used to be, my daddy told me, Sistersville was one of the best places you could live in the whole state. You ask *me* the best place to live, I'd say right where we are, a little four-room house with hills on three sides.

Starting with the innermost circle, students would say the setting is the little four-room house with hills on three sides. Moving outward, they might list the small towns of Sistersville and Friendly on the next two bands before concluding with high up in the hills on an outer band. Of course, you would want to guide a conversation similar to the one you had when you considered the setting of the picture book. Hopefully, the students will see the bigger picture and will conclude that the book is set in a rural area.

What can the reader do independently and collaboratively?

Once your students are familiar with the diagram, give them some blank copies to use on their own. To scaffold them further into the experience, you may suggest they go back and consider the setting of a book they have already read. Having already read the book, they will be familiar with the story and will be able to give the idea of setting more consideration. Encourage them to consider setting in the books they are currently reading after they have had the opportunity to do so in books they have already read.

You might want to encourage older readers to consider how the setting of a book strengthens the book as a whole. Would the book be as wonderful if the setting had not been portrayed the way it had? What kind of research did the author have to conduct to be able to write about such a setting?

What can family members/ caregivers do?

Let family members and caregivers know you are discussing setting with their child in class. Encourage them to do the same at home. Send home blank "Bigger Picture" diagrams with simple, easy-to-follow directions telling how to use them.

We use the following books with rich, descriptive settings:

Peepers by Eve Bunting (2001)
Saturdays and Teacakes by Lester Laminack (2004)
From the Mixed-up Files of Mrs. Basil E. Frankweiler by E. L. Konigsburg (1967)
Charlotte's Web by E. B. White (1952)
The Armadillo from Amarillo by Lynne Cherry (1994)
The Day of Ahmed's Secret by Ted Lewin (1990)

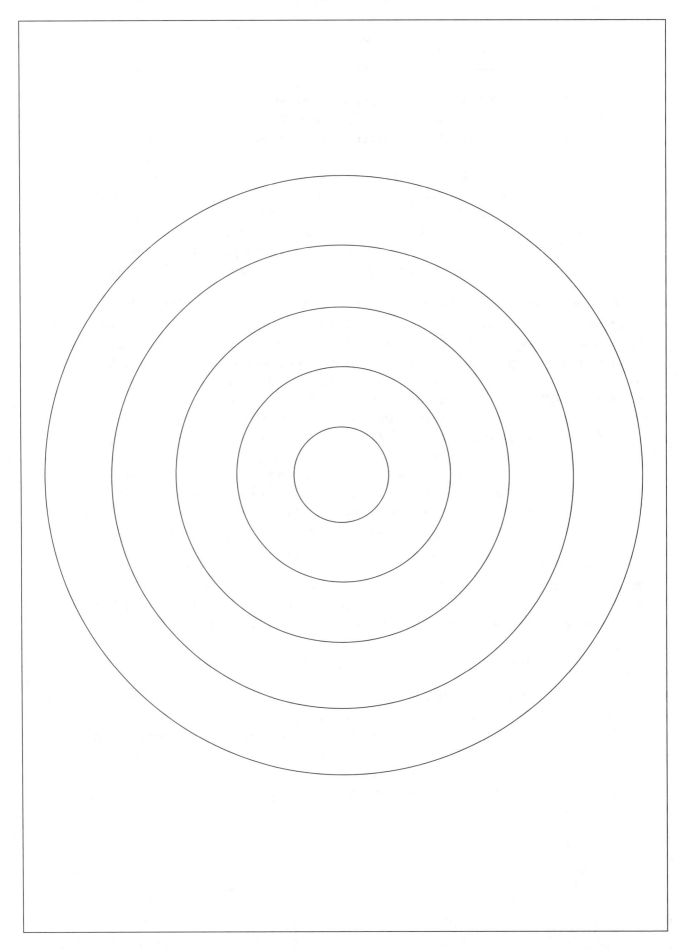

Similes and Metaphors

What do you hear or see?

"Like silent hungry sharks that swim in the darkness of the sea, the German submarines arrived in the middle of the night." These are the words that Theodore Taylor chose to begin his classic book, *The Cay* (1969), and they evoke a powerful picture in your mind. As you look out at your fourth grade class, hoping that they are seeing the same strong images in their minds, a hand shoots up. "I'm lost," a girl confesses, "Are we talking about sharks or submarines?" Other kids share her confusion. "Are the sharks coming to eat them?" another boy asks. The comparison between the hungry sharks and the German U-boats has not registered with the kids. Although you can clearly see the submarines lurking beneath the water like silent, hungry sharks waiting for prey, the kids are totally lost. You decide to take this golden opportunity to explore similes and metaphors.

Why does it matter?

Similes and metaphors are literary devices that permeate text. Similes compare two things using the words *like* or *as*. Metaphors are a bit more challenging. They make comparisons between two dissimilar things by suggesting one thing is really something else. Differentiating between the two is often tricky. These are more difficult to find in picture books, because the authors of these books realize that understanding metaphors requires a degree of abstract thought. Novels and poetry, on the other hand, are more likely to contain metaphors. Many traditional textbooks ask children to identify these devices, but never really explore their purposes. They are key to visualization and are used by authors to evoke powerful mental images and personal connections, both of which are key to comprehension. Although metaphors are a bit more challenging to understand, even the youngest of readers can understand similes. Some similes are so common (as light as a feather, as cool as a cucumber, as fast as lightning) they are almost considered cliché. Understanding the purpose and use of these two literacy devices is vital to deepening comprehension.

What do you do?

Although we do agree it is important that children begin to investigate similes and metaphors by identifying them, we think it is equally important that they immediately begin to analyze the comparison being made. We recognize that this is more art than a skill that takes years and years to refine; however, when given appropriate text examples, we believe that even children in the primary grades can begin to understand these comparisons. We suggest that you explore the devices early and label them as similes and metaphors when appropriate. For the fourth grade class described earlier, it might be time for a formal definition of simile.

Find grade-appropriate examples of similes and metaphors. While novels like *The Cay* obviously contain figurative language, we have found picture books to be equally rich. In *Peepers* by Eve Bunting (2001), she compares a bus with a caterpillar, gravestones with crooked teeth, leaves with toy boats and butterflies, the moon with a pumpkin, and bare trees with brooms sweeping the clouds. This book is perfect to use with students of all ages who are working to use similes and to enhance comprehension.

What can the reader do independently and collaboratively?

- Identify similes and metaphors and elaborate on the comparisons being made. Share this with the group.
- Include similes and metaphors (when appropriate) in their writing.

Skipping Lines

What do you hear or see?

You and a student are seated around a small table in the corner of your classroom. You say a silent prayer, hoping the rest of the class is autonomous enough to work independently for just a few more minutes as you try to squeeze in the assessment of one more student. If all goes well, you will have finished the mandatory assessments and will begin to work on the cumulative report that afternoon after school. You take one last cursory glance around the room, taking time to make sure each student is immersed in some form of reading. You ask the student being assessed to begin and you hold your breath, hoping you can finish before it is time to go to lunch. The student begins to read, everything seems to be going well, you breathe a sigh of relief. Suddenly, what the reader is reading does not correspond with what you are following along with in your assessment binder. Your brain immediately picks up on the discrepancy and is confused for a brief moment before you realize the problem: the student has skipped an entire line of text.

In the assessment-crazed times we teach in, undoubtedly you have spent a great deal of time listening to children read, to assess them either formally or informally. In the case of formal assessments, often the text being read is without illustration and is presented in a straight paragraph format. This can prove to be daunting for the young or struggling reader. Each assessment has its own guidelines or "rules" to follow when a student skips a line. Regardless of what the guidelines are, for you, the teacher, it is painful to witness a child skipping lines of text without realizing it. It is painful because you know that meaning making has been interrupted. Rarely does a reader realize what he has done and attempt to rectify the situation. Instead, he keeps plowing through the text with a lesser understanding of what is being read. Sadly, this happens more often than not in classrooms in which speed of reading is valued more than understanding of what is being read.

Why does it matter?

It is true that proficient readers omit. Goodman, Watson, and Burke (2005) have studied word omissions and Peter Duckett (2002) has completed and published studies on the eye movements of proficient readers. But skipping entire lines of text leads to problems for even the most accomplished reader. In order for the author's meaning to be conveyed, it is important for readers to be aware of three points:

1. They need to read each line of text.
2. They need to realize when they have skipped a line.
3. They need to understand what to do when they do skip a line.

What do you do?

In your meaning-centered classroom, make sure you make readers of all ages and abilities aware of the possibly of skipping lines. Explain to them that this is a mistake that happens to all readers, young and old alike. Skipping the line is not as important as realizing you have skipped the line. Of course, the only way to realize you have skipped a line is to be metacognitively aware of your own meaning-making process to recognize when your comprehension begins to fail.

Go on to tell the students that when they skip a line, the easiest way to rectify the situation is to go back to where they believe the omitted line is (usually the line before the one they just finished) and see if their comprehension becomes more clear with reading it.

After your students are made aware of the potential for skipping lines, make sure you are aware of the possibility of it happening when you listen to students read aloud. It is quite possible you yourself may even skip a line while reading aloud from a favorite picture or chapter book, or while reading over a particularly insightful passage of a textbook. Be ready to catch yourself and know what to do when the miscue occurs. Your students will delight in seeing how you handle the situation!

What can the reader do independently and collaboratively?

Young children who are having difficulty keeping up with multiple lines of text can benefit from a simple straight-edge slip of paper. These slips of paper can be decorated and used as bookmarks. In a very short time, look for them to be used solely as book marks as the young reader becomes more accustomed to reading longer strings of text.

Older students would laugh at the notion of decorating a bookmark, but could just as well be aided by a strip of paper or ruler used to guide them line by line through ever-increasingly longer sections of text. Young and old readers alike also benefit from being reminded that the best utensil to help them follow text can be found at the tip of their index finger.

What can family members/ caregivers do?

Family members and caregivers need to be made aware of the pitfalls of skipping lines. They need to add to the tool chest of strategies they use while reading with their children at home the strategies you have discussed at school. Make sure you keep parents posted by listing strategies in your classroom newsletter, on your classroom website, and so on.

Text Features

**What do you
hear or see?**

Text features (see chart at end of lesson) such as boldface fonts and italics, along with pronunciation guides, foreign phrases, and the like, often pose trouble for readers inexperienced with seeing them. As proficient readers, we know that much of what we encounter reading in our daily living is nonfiction. This text contains the aforementioned features, as well as a host of others. Often, when students do not understand text features, they will skip over them in lieu of using them as keys to help unlock meaning. Inexperienced with these features, readers often overlook them or deem them unnecessary to comprehension.

**Why does
it matter?**

Understanding text features and being able to use them to their fullest potential is critical to understanding the great amounts of nonfiction reading we encounter throughout our lives as readers. For primary-age children, text features show up in the nonfiction reading they do as they complete theme immersions, and study various cultures and aspects of life. Just open a *Time for Kids* magazine and the text features nearly leap off the page at you. This can be quite daunting for the younger reader who has no idea how to traverse them. Text features become more prevalent in the middle and upper grades as assigned texts become more content driven and more nonfiction resources are used.

**What do
you do?**

When you come to a particular text feature in any genre, do not automatically assume that students understand what it is used for and what it means. Make sure you point out text features to your students and make them aware of their uses. Multiple classroom copies of periodicals such as *Time for Kids, Sports Illustrated for Kids, Scholastic News,* and the like serve this purpose well. Put the mandatory textbooks in your classroom to good use with older students. Use them to demonstrate the power of understanding text features.

Regardless of the age student you work with, consider doing a ministudy of text features in your classroom. This study can be easily incorporated into nonfiction writing composed by the students. When developing a rubric to assess the writing, maybe include various text features and how they were woven into the nonfiction piece.

Maintain a display of oversized, student-created examples of text features in your classroom. These examples may come from reading done by either you or the students. Make sure to encourage the students to include a definition of the particular feature, how it is used, and where it might be found. If a classroom display is too cumbersome or awkward, keep examples bound in a small book kept within handy reach with other classroom library reference books.

What can the reader do independently and collaboratively?

Readers might keep a running tally of which text features they encounter as they read. The class may possibly be able to determine which ones are most prevalent. Readers might also keep track of examples of text features encountered across the curriculum.

Long after a study of text features is completed, continue to encourage students to insert them into their writing. Aid them in understanding that text features help the reader gain meaning from the text.

What can family members/ caregivers do?

Keep family members and caregivers abreast of your study of text features in class. Encourage them to point out text features as they are reading with younger children or studying with older children. Propose the challenge of finding examples of text features different than those found in class.

Text Feature	Science	Social Studies	Mathematics	Reading
Bold face font				
Italics				
Underlining				
Bullets • ✓				
Pronunciation guides				
Graphs/ charts				
Margin notations				

Examples of Text Features in Fiction and Nonfiction

Text Feature	Fiction Example	Nonfiction Example
Font style: italics, boldface, and so on	*The Amazing Days of Abby Hayes: Every Cloud Has a Silver Lining* (Mazer, 2000) adeptly shows the power and popularity of various fonts being used to convey meaning in text. Each book of this popular intermediate chapter book series is full of varying fonts. A good example from this particular book is the school supply list Abby ponders at the beginning of chapter two on page 11. The supply list is shown in boldface type, and Abby's candid remarks about each item are written in purple italic letters. This is a perfect minilesson to demonstrate how font style is used to show the real feelings of a character. In the 2005 Newbery Honor book, *Lizzie Bright and the Buckminster Boy* (Schmidt, 2004), words are written in italics to	In *Martin's Big Words,* author Doreen Rappaport (2001) and illustrator Bryan Collier use an obviously large font to highlight quotes from some of Martin Luther King, Jr.'s most popular speeches. The quotations are shown along with the biographical storyline of the powerful book. Most often, textbooks of all subject matters include key words in boldface font. Often, these words are included in a glossary at the back of the book. Incorporate a textbook from a content area into a minilesson about boldface words.

Text Feature	Fiction Example	Nonfiction Example
Font style: italics, boldface, and so on (*Continued*)	show great emphasis. On page 99, Turner, one of the main characters, is scolded sternly by his very strict father, who says, "*Forbidden* is *forbidden*. You will stay in the house for the next two weeks, Turner." Boldface words are used in the picture book *Sometimes My Mommy Gets Angry* written by Bebe Moore Campbell (2003) and illustrated by E. B. Lewis.	
Captions/voice bubbles	The end papers of Doreen Cronin's *Diary of a Spider* (2005) are filled with snapshots of the spider's life. Underneath each square snapshot is a caption describing it. More and more, illustrators are using the end papers of the book as space to include more artwork. (The end papers are literally the first and last pages of the book. This includes the pages that are glued to the inside and backside covers.) Readers need to	Newspapers of all varieties are full of captions underneath the many pictures they include in their stories. These captions are often brief and to the point. They offer the struggling reader a vehicle to understanding better what the entire article is about. Newspapers are an inexpensive means to show students many text features. Periodicals, both for adults and children,

Text Feature	Fiction Example	Nonfiction Example
Captions/voice bubbles (*Continued*)	be made aware of the sometimes-impressive art that covers these pages. The reader skipping over them in *Diary of a Spider* is missing out on a great deal of humor. What would a spider's favorite book be? *Charlotte's Web*, of course! Baby pictures, first web pictures, and the like are included. Cronin also makes use of voice bubbles in the book as well. Voice bubbles are the comic book-style balloons that appear over characters' heads that show what they are thinking or speaking. As with other features of text, these need to be pointed out to the reader because they often carry significant meaning and insight into the characters and plot.	contain captions near the pictures they are referring to. Readers may need to be shown that sometimes in a periodical, the caption is near or around the picture it is describing. It is not always found underneath it, like they are in newspapers. A list of magazines for children can be found at the end of this book.
Charts, diagrams, and labels	Who can forget the first time they saw the labeled diagram of the newborn baby in Jamie Lee Curtis' *Tell Me Again about the Night I Was Born* (1996)?	Gail Gibbons is best known for her nonfiction picture books about innumerable topics. Her subject matter spans every topic, from the

Text Feature	Fiction Example	Nonfiction Example
Charts, diagrams, and labels (*Continued*)	This book, based on the real-life adoption experience of the author is a favorite of children of all ages. The labeled diagram is shown actual size when you spin the book around and look at the illustration vertically. Cradle cap, the forming belly button, wrinkles, and so forth, are each labeled in the diagram. This is a whimsical way to guide students through the aspects of a diagram. *Aneesa Lee and the Weaver's Gift* (Grimes, 1999) depicts a labeled diagram of a loom on page 3 of the book just before this collection of poems by Nikki Grimes about the art of weaving and the weaver herself begins. Artist Ashley Bryan adeptly shows the many intricate parts of the loom in his beautiful illustration. A chart is used to convey further an important lesson in the 1962 Newbery Award-winning	history of holidays to farm animals. Each one is full of rich examples of text features found across the genre of nonfiction. Her books can be used with young readers who delve into their content with great enthusiasm. Older readers could be introduced to nonfiction text features using the simple, easy-to-understand examples found in Gibbons's work. The examples discussed here come from *Behold . . . The Dragons!* (1999). In this book about the mythical beasts that many children find intriguing, a detailed diagram of a Chinese dragon is included. This diagram labels each part of the dragon and tells what each part actually is. For example, the "stag antlers" are labeled in parentheses with the more common name "horns." There is a pronunciation guide, as well!

Text Feature	Fiction Example	Nonfiction Example
Charts, diagrams, and labels (*Continued*)	classic, *A Wrinkle in Time*. In the book, author Madeleine L'Engle attempts to explain the scientific phenomenon of time travel. She uses the character Mrs. Whatsit to explain the theory of tesseracting through time. In order for the reader to understand the concept fully, a diagram of the example being given is included.	
Headings, glossary, table of contents, index, prologue, epilogue	Sometimes a work of fiction is divided into sections. Nancy Farmer's *The House of the Scorpion* (2002) is a chapter book divided into concise sections. Each section details a period in the life of the main character. First-time readers of such a large work of fiction may find comfort in tackling one section at a time instead of looking at the book as a whole. *Aneesa Lee and the Weaver's Gift* has a glossary at the front. Entitled "Weaving Words," the glossary	Any textbook, regardless of the content area, will have headings, a glossary, a table of contents, and an index. Bring out the math book during reading workshop and spend some time looking carefully at the headings of each part, chapter, and section of the book. Students will begin to realize that headings play a crucial role in organizing the subject matter at hand. Encourage them to use the table of contents and index to find the sections of the book they believe hold answers to the

Text Feature	Fiction Example	Nonfiction Example
Headings, glossary, table of contents, index, prologue, epilogue (*Continued*)	contains words from *beater* to *weft* and must be important given its place at the front of the book before any of the poems begin. So often we have encountered students who view the prologue and epilogue of a book as "free pages" they are entitled to skip. This is not the case. A perfect book to bring this fact to their attention is Natalie Babbitt's classic, *Tuck Everlasting* (1975). The prologue deftly sets up the book and its main characters. Readers will find themselves clamoring to read the epilogue of the book to find out what critical choice the main character has finally made. Not to read the epilogue is not to know how the book ends.	questions they have. Have them compare the ways their math and social studies texts are organized. Encourage them to look for similarities and differences. Textbooks also use a glossary to aid student comprehension. Although we are not advocates of mindless vocabulary drills and activities, we do want our students to understand the ability of the glossary to support their comprehension. Should they not be able to understand a word from the context within which it is used, they need to know the glossary is there to help them out.

Themes and Morals

What do you hear or see?

You have just finished reading aloud Sarah Stewart's picture book *The Friend* (2004) to your fifth grade class. The poignant, touching, deeply moving last line is still hanging in the air and you notice several students in your class are beginning to line up for PE class. Mortified, you ask them why and they reply like only a fifth grader can, "Because it's PE time." Undaunted by their sarcasm, you let them know that after PE you are going to be discussing the book in more detail.

What happened? Does the situation sound familiar? Have you found yourself in the starring role of this scenario? As teachers, we all have. You pour your heart, soul, and every drop of emotion into the reading and sharing of a book to find its reception less than lackluster. Why is this the case? We believe that readers need practice being able to recognize the theme or moral behind a story. Not always gleaned from the surface level, sometimes the theme and moral are lurking far below.

Why does it matter?

Students' ability to determine the theme or moral of a book is vital to their understanding the author's purpose. The theme or moral is the proverbial lesson the book is trying to teach us to consider and ponder. Knowing how to find out the theme or moral of a book gives readers of all ages the keys to a much deeper understanding.

What do you do?

- Teachers everywhere are challenged by the need to encourage their students to think more deeply. In our increasingly fast-paced society, taking the time to slow down and think is often not on the minds of our students. Take baby steps into helping your students consider theme and moral. Regardless of their age, start small and grow from there.
- You may begin a discussion of theme or moral before reading a book. As you preview the book and make predictions with the class, ask them to be thinking about what the author "really wants us to know." "Why do you think the author wrote this book? What lesson do they hope readers will come away with?" Hopefully these questions will cause them to begin thinking as they read or hear the book for the first time.
- Of course, the first theme or moral many students encounter is the one of "And they all lived happily ever after." A beautiful notion, but one we know is not quite right as students become older, more proficient readers. Persuade your students to dig deeper into the book as they think about the theme or moral. Mem Fox's simply told tale *Koala Lou* (1989b) poses an excellent opportunity to discuss theme and moral. Questions such as "What is Koala Lou worried about? Why can't her

mother give her the attention she once could?" will serve as the perfect beginning to a discussion about theme and moral.

- Another simply told classic book with an easy-to-identify theme or moral is *Swimmy* by Leo Lionni (1968). In *Swimmy*, the themes of cooperation and individuality are celebrated together as a school of fish learns to live together, recognizing there is a place for everyone in this world.

- The work of Eve Bunting always contains a strong message. Older readers will find her books interesting and often mesmerizing. Bunting deals with contemporary social issues that many children's authors shy away from. With a sensitive and graceful style, Bunting attacks the issues head on. In *The Memory String* (2000), Bunting tells the tale of a young girl who, while still mourning the death of her mother, finds herself having to begin a new life with her father's new wife.

- Older students may be interested in comparing and contrasting the terms *theme* and *moral*. How are they alike? How are they different?

What can the reader do independently and collaboratively?

- Readers can help create a theme and moral log for use in their journals. Of course, you wouldn't want them to track the theme and moral of every book they read in a year, but while spotlighting theme and moral in your mini- or whole-class lessons, it might prove to be wise. A sample of what the log might look like is included at the end of this lesson.

- Encourage older readers to practice determining theme by using picture books. Picture books are much shorter and less cumbersome to read than chapter books. Thus, they allow more time and provide more opportunities for readers to consider themes and morals.

- After students have experience discussing and considering themes and morals, have them group books into common themes. An interesting theme for students to consider is one about themselves. Nobody knows you better than you do! Clark expanded the idea he learned while an undergraduate in college. Then-professor Roberta Long had each of her children's literature students build a collection of children's books that reflected them, their interests, and so forth.

- To this day, Clark begins each school year by showing his basket of books that tell about him. His basket includes a collection of poetry, *Sing to the Sun* (1992) by his favorite author/illustrator, Ashley Bryan. He includes a chapter book he is currently reading, *Flush* (2005) by Carl Hiaasen, and a fiction picture book celebrating his Norwegian heritage, *Uff Da!* (Martin, 2004). A type I diabetic most of his life, Clark's basket also includes a nonfiction piece, *Taking Diabetes to School* (Gosselin, 1998), about diabetes. These titles simply name a few. The basket is part of the classroom environment and is read from and added to throughout the year.

- Students could also create theme or moral collections consisting of books with a similar theme or moral. Themes and morals could be brainstormed ahead of time by the class and they could add the book physically to a collection or write it down on a classroom chart or literature log data sheet. An example of one is included at the end of this lesson.

What can family members/ caregivers do? In our complex society, many family members and caregivers are concerned about the morals life has to offer their young children. Children's literature provides a vast collection of books that have morals of all sorts. Encourage family members and caregivers to utilize the examples of outstanding characters set forth in children's literature.

Some of our favorite books for discussing morals and themes include:

The Printer by Myron Uhlberg (2003)
The Summer My Father Was Ten by Pat Brisson (1998)
Bootsie Barker Bites by Barbara Bottner (1992)
Things That Sometimes Happen by Avi (1970)
Riding Freedom by Pam Munoz Ryan (1998)

Themes and Morals

Theme or moral	Which book was it found in?	Page number	Example to support your thinking

Underprediction/Wild Guesses

carton-
car-

realized-
really-

sound-

Miscue: Walking toward the cave, the man felt relief having finally found shelter from the storm.

What do you hear or see?

While reading with a middle school-age student, you notice her underprediction of words. Sometimes this underpredicting of words is referred to as *wild guessing,* alluding to the notion that she is simply guessing haphazardly while paying no attention to constructing meaning. Underprediction occurs in readers who view reading as a chore to complete, an arduous task to finish for the teacher. Readers who underpredict simply want to finish what has been given to them to read so they can go back to other activities they enjoy more.

Why does it matter?

As teachers, we wish for our students, regardless of their age, to possess a deep appreciation and love of reading. We want them to value literacy in the same ways we do. Although we model and demonstrate our love of reading daily in our classrooms, there is always a student or two we feel we are not connecting with. This concern is paramount for teachers of older students. Often, by the time underpredictive students reach middle or high school, they have encountered numerous interactions with print that have been less than pleasant. They have not been nurtured to become readers. They view reading as one of the many tasks they must complete simply to "get by" or "get through" school.

What do you do?

We hope that astute middle and high school teachers will be on the lookout for readers who are underpredictive and who make wild guesses as they read. As soon as this behavior is recognized, an intense intervention must begin. Reading must be presented to the underpredictive student in another light. Convinced they cannot read well and sure they don't like to read for pleasure, students such as these need to be made aware that reading is indeed a pleasurable activity. Finding reading material that suits their interests is an excellent place to begin. Sometimes, as the teacher, you may need to broaden your definition of reading. Reading, after all, does encompass more than Chaucer's classic *Canterbury Tales* (Cohen, 1998) and Homer's *The Odyssey* (Lattimore, 1967). Books of all sorts, genres, and lengths should be celebrated in middle and high school classrooms. Periodicals, newspapers, pamphlets, and the like, revolving around students' interests are invaluable in proving the point to them that reading is indeed a pleasurable activity. Look for ways to teach, model, and practice strategies with your students within texts they find interesting. With the Internet at the finger-tips of more and more classroom teachers and reading specialists, student-specific text is becoming easier and easier to locate and utilize.

What can the reader do independently and collaboratively? Students who find reading a chore need to be encouraged to consider topics they find interesting. Be wary of overwhelming them with too lengthy an interest inventory because they will most likely feel intimidated and not be as honest with themselves, and you, as you would hope them to be. A simple example of an inventory is included at the end of this lesson.

What can family members/ caregivers do? Just like the teacher who needs to broaden her definition of reading, very often families need to be encouraged to do so at home. Without prying or casting judgment, see if you can find out how literacy is valued or not valued in the home. Questions to consider include the following:

- Do any family members read?
- Do they read for pleasure?
- What do they read?
- Are there any reading materials in the house?
- Does the house have access to the Internet or a local library?
- Has reading been made a task or job the child must complete?

A sure way of making reading unpleasant is to "assign" a specific time to read. Clark and Shelly have both heard many parents with the best of intentions say at the end of a school year, "And we plan to read 45 minutes every single day this summer!" Why not simply value the moments spent reading to a young child before they drift off to sleep or the time spent with an older child reading and discussing a treasured comic book collection? Are children's interests being taken into account when reading material is being selected?

Interest Inventory

Name: _____   Date: _____

List 5 things you wish you knew more about.	List 5 places you wish you could travel.
List 5 things you like to do.	List 5 people you would like to meet.

Using Illustration to Aid Comprehension of a Nonlinear Plot

What do you hear or see?

You notice a reader with a picture book you know to have a nonlinear plot. Because the plot does not follow the anticipated beginning–middle–end formula, you are concerned the reader may not be comprehending the text as well as she should. You wonder if she is using the illustrations to help her better understand what she is reading.

Why does it matter?

Readers of all ages and abilities need to know that the illustrations of a picture book are there to help support the story. The illustrations and the writing work hand in hand to help the reader comprehend the message the author and/or illustrator is trying to relay. Readers often realize this strategy, but do not use it to its fullest potential.

What do you do?

Find examples of picture books in which the illustrations help support a nonlinear plot. A classic example is Maurice Sendak's Caldecott Award-winning book of 1963, *Where the Wild Things Are*. As Max leaves the comfort and security of his personal reality and begins to enter the land of the Wild Things, the illustrations grow. The illustrations grow to consume two double-page spreads, depicting the wild rumpus. Similarly, as Max returns to the comfort and security of his world, the illustrations become smaller and smaller. Sendak brilliantly uses the size of the illustrations to help scaffold the reader to a deeper understanding.

A more recent example is Allen Say's book, *Kamishibai Man* (2005b). Say, known for his carefully painted, exact, precise method of illustration, uses a change in style to reflect a twist in a nonlinear plot. In the book, the Kamishibai man is a gentleman who tells stories to children and adults. He tells his story strictly for the pleasure of doing so. He travels on a bicycle with a small "stage" added to the back. On this stage, he displays story cards that guide his oral renderings. Say makes this very obvious to the reader when the Kamishibai man in his book begins to weave his tale. You notice the illustration switches from Say's traditional style to one more cartoon- and childlike. When the Kamishibai man is finished telling his story, the illustration switches back to Say's more characteristic style.

By pointing out these specific examples, you will bring the importance of utilizing the illustrator's work to its fullest potential to the forefront for the reader. Like text features, they are important to understanding what is being read as a whole.

What can the reader do independently and collaboratively?

Readers may want to keep a listing of books in which they used the illustrations to help them understand what is being read.

What can family members/ caregivers do?

Family members and caregivers need to be aware of the importance of illustration in children's literature. They need to understand the important place illustrations hold in the overall comprehension of the text. By sending home information about the American Library Association's prestigious Caldecott Award, you will help educate them in the importance of illustrations in children's literature.

Parents of older children as well as parents of children who have crossed the threshold into being able to read independently need to be assured that their children can still read a picture book. So often, after a child is able to read independently, parents believe (with good intentions) that their child should be reading the biggest, thickest book they can possibly find. Not so. Many picture books are meant for a much more sophisticated reader. Take a look at Peter Sis's *Tibet through the Red Box* (1998) and you will see for yourself how complicated a seemingly simple picture book can be.

Visualization

What do you hear or see?

When conferring with a student about her self-selected text, you notice that she confuses many of the characters and elements of the plot. When you encourage her to retell the story and describe the characters and setting, she is unable to do so. You begin to suspect that she is not visualizing as she reads.

Why does it matter?

Good readers often describe visualization as a movie in the mind. We have all gone to see our favorite novel brought to life on the big screen, only to be disappointed when the protagonist does not look a thing like she did in our mind's eye. As we visualize a text, we make deeper connections to it on all levels and are better able to follow and recall the elements of the story. Visualizing is essential to rich comprehension. Many struggling readers, as well as children who claim to hate reading, also report that they do not visualize as they read.

What do you do?

Give visualization the attention it deserves and do not assume that all children do it as naturally as you almost certainly do. Explain the act and importance of visualizing, and provide readers with many opportunities to share their mental images with you. Children are often encouraged to write about their reading in a response journal. We believe that children should also be encouraged to draw about their reading.

Obviously, authors visualize their stories as they write them. Authors who illustrate their own words are able to share those visualizations with us. Authors who do not illustrate often see the visualizations of others accompany their words. Children are often amazed to find that authors do not have total control of the illustrations that accompany the text.

Share many descriptive texts with your students. If the text is accompanied by beautiful illustrations, hide them from sight. Ask your students to draw what they have seen in their minds as you read. You may then assess the drawings to see if they reflect anything close to the image the text was attempting to create. Poetry is especially powerful, as each word is carefully chosen to evoke a powerful image. Shelly recently conducted a visualization lesson with a group of fifth graders using a poem that describes a coming blizzard. She asked the students to fold a sheet of plain paper in half, labeling one half "first stanza" and the other half "second stanza." As the poem unfolds, the image of a snowy day is transformed into a blizzard of pink petals that are falling from an "invisible cloud." On most sheets, the first stanza evoked gray images and snowflakes, while the second stanza evoked images of fluffy trees and drifts of pink petals. Although it took repeated reads, the students' visualizations were impressive, considering the fact that these students had never seen an appreciable snowfall, let alone a blizzard. Although the drawings were amazingly similar, no two were alike. This point was used to illustrate the fact that no two schemas are exactly the same, and therefore, no two people will visualize a text in exactly the same way.

You might also host a screening of a movie that is based on a novel you have explored together. Although teachers often engage in such activities, we have found that children are typically asked to compare and contrast the movie and the book. We encourage you to instead ask the students to compare their visualizations of the characters and settings with those in the book. Sometimes, like you and your students, we are left to wonder whether the movie makers even read the novel!

What can the reader do independently and collaboratively?	• Ask the reader to sketch visualizations from books or poetry in his or her reading response journal or writer's notebook.
	• Allow children to sketch and draw during read-alouds.
	• Encourage the students to share their drawings and visualizations with each other.
	• Ask pairs of students to collaborate on a drawing of a single text or poem. The exchange of ideas and social interaction will no doubt elicit more powerful visualizations.
	• Put blank paper in the listening center and ask children to draw elements from the book based on their visualizations.
	• Write single words that evoke powerful mental images on index cards: *juicy, jagged, sizzling, freezing, lively, solid,* and so forth. Have students choose a card at random and draw their visualizations elicited by the word.

| **What can family members/ caregivers do?** | • Listen and provide appropriate, supportive feedback. |
| | • Read aloud together and share your visualizations. |

Wild Guesses

What do you hear or see?

While listening to a child read, you note that when she encounters words that she does not immediately recognize, she appears to take wild guesses, substituting words that almost certainly impede comprehension.

Why does it matter?

These wild guesses *might* be a sign that the student is focused on a single phonetic cue and is consequently guessing at the remaining sounds. Overly predictive readers often appear to be guessing wildly about words, whereas in actuality they are attempting to use an underdeveloped word-solving strategy. These readers simply place too much emphasis on the initial phonetic cue and often insert the first word that pops into their minds. On the other hand, underpredictive readers appear to use none of the phonetic cues and substitute words that have no resemblance to those in the actual text.

In both cases, if there are a lot of miscues that involve meaning changes, this is indicative of a reader who is stuck at a very textual level of reading and does not self-monitor or understand that reading is thinking. It is important to note that as children grow as readers and encounter more complex phonetic patterns, it is also possible that they recognize the initial or final sound, but give up on the medial vowels. Many older, struggling readers have reported they "panic" when they see "lots of vowels in a word," and "just say something."

What do you do?

Conduct a thorough miscue analysis to determine the needs of the reader. The presence of wild guesses and/or the absence of self-corrections are red flags. If the reader is overly predictive,

- Read the miscue analysis text aloud to the student, using the student's miscues. Ask the student to stop you if the text does not make sense. This will allow you to determine whether the reader can monitor her own listening comprehension.
- Reflect on the miscues with the student and discuss possible reasons for them. Ask her to suggest words that would help the text make sense. Model substituting these words.
- Select a few words from the text. Remind the reader to look at every sound in the word and practice reading words all the way to the end.

If the reader is underpredictive,

- Read the miscue analysis text aloud to the student, using the student's miscues. Ask her to stop you if the text does not make sense. This will allow you to determine whether the reader can monitor her own listening comprehension.
- Reflect on the miscues with the student and discuss possible reasons for them. Ask the reader to suggest words that would help the text make sense. Model substituting words.
- Select a few words from the text. Remind the reader that the sounds in the words she reads should match the letters on the page. Practice reading words all the way to the end.

If gaps in the graphophonic cueing system are noted, those gaps should be filled. Explicitly teach students how to handle the cues that are troublesome and provide much guided and independent practice doing so.

Make "Is this making sense?" the class mantra. Help the reader recognize when meaning breaks down. This will force the reader to take a second look at the text. When self-corrections begin to appear in running records and miscue analyses, you will know the reader is growing.

What can the reader do independently and collaboratively?

- Let the student record herself reading short texts. Have her listen to her reading, checking to see if what she hears makes sense. Ask her to listen to the reading a second time, seeing if she can identify the words that caused the break in meaning. Allow her to record herself a second time.
- Be sure that the reader is engaged with text at an appropriate level during independent reading.

What can family members/ caregivers do?

- Share the class mantra "Is this making sense?" with family members and caregivers. Ask them to listen to the child read, asking that question when necessary.
- Remind caregivers to give readers the opportunity to solve their own reading dilemmas. Simply telling kids words they miss makes them more dependent as readers. Reminding them to think about words that would make sense and showing them how to match that thinking to the printed word will lead to independent readers.

Recommended Children's Literature

Books

Abbott, Tony. 2002. *The Secrets of Droon: The Magic Escapes*. New York: Scholastic.

Altman, Linda Jacobs. 1999. *Amelia's Road*. Boston: Houghton Mifflin.

Avi. 1970. *Things That Sometimes Happen*. New York: Antheneum Books.

Babbitt, Natalie. 1975. *Tuck Everlasting*. New York: Farrar, Straus, Giroux.

Ballard, Robert D. 1988. *Exploring the Titanic*. Toronto: Madison Press.

Baylor, Byrd. 1978. *The Way to Start a Day*. New York: Scribner's.

———. 1986. *I'm in Charge of Celebrations*. New York: Scribner's.

———. 1998. *The Table Where Rich People Sit*. New York: Aladdin Paperbacks.

Beaumont, Karen. 2005. *I Ain't Gonna Paint No More!* Orlando, FL: Harcourt.

Bloom, Becky. 1999. *Wolf!* New York: Orchard Books.

Borden, Louise. *The A+ Custodian*. New York: Simon & Schuster.

Bottner, Barbara. 1992. *Bootsie Barker Bites*. New York: G. P. Putman's Sons.

Brisson, Pat. 1998. *The Summer My Father Was Ten*. Honesdale, PA: Boyds Mills Press.

Bruchac, Joseph. 1994. *A Boy Called Slow*. New York: Philomel Books.

Bryan, Ashley. 1992. *Sing to the Sun: Poems and Pictures*. New York: HarperCollins.

Buehner, Caralyn. 2004. *Superdog the Heart of a Hero*. New York: HarperCollins.

Bunting, Eve. 1991. *Fly Away Home*. New York: Clarion Books.

———. 1994a. *A Day's Work*. New York: Clarion Books.

———. 1994b. *Smoky Night*. San Diego: Harcourt Brace.

———. 2000. *The Memory String*. New York: Clarion Books.

———. 2001. *Peepers*. San Diego: Harcourt.

Campbell, Bebe Moore. 2003. *Sometimes My Mommy Gets Angry*. New York: G. P. Putnam's Sons.

Carle, Eric. 1969. *The Very Hungry Caterpillar*. New York: Philomel Books.

Cherry, Lynne. 1994. *The Armadillo from Amarillo*. New York: Gulliver Green.

Chinn, Karen. 1999. *Sam and the Lucky Money*. Boston: Houghton Mifflin.

Choldenko, Gennifer. 2004. *Al Capone Does My Shirts*. New York: G.P. Putnam's Sons.

Cohen, Barbara. 1988. *Canterbury Tales*. New York: Lothrop, Lee & Shepard Books.

Cole, Joanna, and Bruce Degen. *The Magic School Bus Series*. New York: Scholastic.

———. 2005. *Mrs. Frizzle's Adventure Series: Imperial China*. New York: Scholastic.

Cowley, Joy. 1998. *Big Moon Tortilla*. Honesdale: Boyds Mills Press.

Creech, Sharon. 2000. *The Wanderer*. New York: HarperCollins.

Cronin, Doreen. 2005. *Diary of a Spider*. New York: Joanna Cotler Books.

Curtis, Jamie Lee. 1996. *Tell Me Again About the Night I Was Born*. New York: HarperCollins.

Dahl, Roald. 1998. *Charlie and the Chocolate Factory*. New York: Puffin Books.

DiCamillo, Kate. 2000. *Because of Winn-Dixie*. Cambridge, MA: Candlewick.

Donnelly, Judy. 1987. *The Titanic, Lost and Found*. New York: Random House.

Duvoisin, Robert. [1950] 1977. *Petunia*. New York: Knopf.

Dykes, Tomoko Tsuchiya. 1988. *Faithful Elephants*. Boston: Houghton Mifflin.

Farmer, Nancy. 2002. *The House of the Scorpion*. New York: Atheneum Books for Young Readers.

Fleischman, Paul. 1999. *Weslandia*. Cambridge, MA: Candlewick Press.

Fletcher, Ralph J. 1995. *Fig Pudding*. New York: Clarion Books.

Florian, Doug. 1996. *Bing, Bang, Boing*. New York: Penguin Young Readers.

Fox, Mem. 1989a. *Feathers and Fools*. San Diego: Harcourt Brace Jovanovich.

———. 1989b. *Koala Lou*. San Diego: Harcourt Brace Jovanovich.

Garland, Sherry. 2000. *Voices of the Alamo*. New York: Scholastic.

Gerstein, Mordicai. 2003. *The Man Who Walked between the Towers*. New York: Scholastic.

Gibbons, Gail. 1989. *Catch the Wind!* Boston: Little, Brown and Company.

———. 1999. *Behold . . . the Dragons!* New York: Morrow Junior Books.

Gosselin, Kim. 1998. *Taking Diabetes to School.* Valley Park, MO: JayJo Books.

Grimes, Nikki. 1999. *Aneesa Lee and the Weaver's Gift.* New York: Lothrop, Lee & Shepard.

Hanson, Warren. 1997. *The Next Place.* Minneapolis, MN: Waldman House Press.

Hiaasen, Carl. 2005. *Flush.* New York: Alfred A. Knopf.

Holm, Jennifer L. 1999. *Our Only May Amelia.* New York: HarperCollins.

Jacobs, Linda. 1993. *Amelia's Road.* New York: Lee and Low.

Karas, G. Brian. 2002. *Atlantic.* New York: G.P. Putnam's Sons.

Kerley, Barbara. 2001. *The Dinosaurs of Waterhouse Hawkins.* New York: Scholastic.

———. 2004. *Walt Whitman: Words for America.* New York: Scholastic.

Kidder, Tracy. 2003. *Mountains Beyond Mountains.* New York: Random House.

Konigsburg, E. L. 1967. *From the Mixed-up Files of Mrs. Basil E. Frankweiler.* New York: Antheneum.

———. 2004. *The Outcasts of 19 Schuyler Place.* New York: Simon & Schuster.

Kunhardt, Dorothy. 1976. *Pat the Bunny.* Racine, WI: Golden Press.

Laminack, Lester. 2004. *Saturdays and Teacakes.* Atlanta: Peachtree.

Lattimore, Deborah Nourse. 1994. *Frida Maria.* New York: Harcourt Brace.

Lattimore, Richmond Alexander. 1967. *The Odyssey of Homer.* New York: Harper & Row.

L'Engle, Madeleine. 1962. *A Wrinkle in Time.* New York: Ariel Books.

Levine, Gail Carson. 1997. *Ella Enchanted.* New York: Scholastic.

Lewin, Ted. 1990. *The Day of Ahmed's Secret.* New York: Lothrop, Lee & Shepard Books.

———. 2001. *Red Legs.* New York: HarperCollins.

———. 2002. *Big Jimmy's Kum Kau Chinese Take Out.* New York: HarperCollins.

Lionni, Leo. 1968. *Swimmy.* New York: Pantheon.

Locker, Thomas. 1997. *Water Dance.* Orlando: Harcourt.

Lyon, George Ella. 1991. *Cecil's Story.* New York: Orchard Books.

Marcellino, Fred. 1999. *I Crocodile.* New York: HarperCollins.

Martin, C. L. G. 2004. *Úff da!* Berkeley, CA: Tricycle Press.

Martin, Jacqueline Briggs. 1998. *Snowflake Bentley.* Boston: Houghton Mifflin.

Mazer, Anne. 2000. *The Amazing Days of Abby Hayes: Every Cloud Has a Silver Lining.* New York: Scholastic.

McGill, Alice. 1999. *Molly Bannaky.* Boston, MA: Houghton Mifflin.

Morrison, Toni, and Slade Morrison. 1999. *The Big Box*. New York: Hyperion Books for Children.

Myers, Christopher. 1999. *Black Cat*. New York: Scholastic.

Naylor, Phyllis Reynolds. 1991. *Shiloh*. New York: Atheneum.

Park, Linda Sue. 2005. *Project Mulberry: A Novel*. New York: Clarion Books.

Paul, Ann Whitford. 2004. *Manana, Iguana*. New York: Scholastic.

Paterson, Katherine. 1977. *Bridge to Terabithia*. New York: Crowell.

Peck, Richard. 1998. *A Long Way from Chicago*. New York: Dial Books for Young Readers.

———. 2000. *A Year down Yonder*. New York: Dial Books for Young Readers.

———. 2004. *The Teacher's Funeral: A Comedy in Three Parts*. New York: Dial Books.

Polacco, Patricia. 1992. *Chicken Sunday*. New York: Philomel Books.

Raschka, Chris. 1998. *Arlene Sardine*. New York: Orchard Books.

Rappaport, Doreen. 2001. *Martin's Big Words*. New York: Hyperion Books for Children.

Raven, Margot Theis. 2002. *Mercedes and the Chocolate Pilot*. Chelsea, MI: Sleeping Bear Press.

Rosen, Michael. 1989. *We're Going on a Bear Hunt*. New York: Margaret K. McElderry Books.

Royston, Angela. 2001. *Screws*. Chicago: Heinemann.

Ryan, Pam Munoz. 1998. *Riding Freedom*. New York: Scholastic.

———. 2000. *Esperanza Rising*. New York: Scholastic.

———. 2005. *Becoming Naomi Leon*. New York: Scholastic.

Sachar, Louis. 1984. *Holes*. New York: Farrar, Straus, Giroux.

San Souci, Robert D. 1995. *Kate Shelly Bound for Legend*. New York: Dial.

Say, Allen. 1997. *Allison*. Boston: Houghton Mifflin.

———. 2005a. *Emma's Rug*. Boston: Houghton Mifflin.

———. 2005b. *Kamishibai Man*. Boston: Houghton Mifflin.

Sendak, Maurice. 1963. *Where the Wild Things Are*. New York: Harper & Row.

Schaefer, Lola M. 2004. *Arrowhawk*. New York: Henry Holt and Company.

Schmidt, Gary D. 2004. *Lizzie Bright and the Buckminster Boy*. New York: Clarion Books.

Scieszka, Jon. 1998. *The True Story of the Three Little Pigs*. New York: Puffin Books.

Silverstein, Shel. 1974. *Where the Sidewalk Ends: The Poems and Drawings of Shel Silverstein*. New York: HarperCollins.

Sis, Peter. 1998. *Tibet: Through the Red Box*. New York: Farrar, Straus, & Giroux.

Sorensen, Henri. 1995. *New Hope*. New York: Lothrop, Lee, & Shepard.

Spillsbury, Louise, and Richard. 2005. *Sweeping Tsunamis*. Chicago: Heinemann.

Spinelli, Eileen. 2004. *Something to Tell the Grandcows*. Grand Rapids, MI: Eerdman's Books for Young Readers.

Spinelli, Jerry. 2002. *Loser*. New York: HarperCollins.

Stevens, Janet. 1995. *Tops & Bottoms*. New York: Scholatstic.

Stewart, Sarah. 1991. *The Money Tree*. New York: Farrar, Straus, & Giroux.

———. 1997. *The Gardener*. New York: Farrar, Straus, & Giroux.

———. 2004. *The Friend*. New York: Farrar, Straus, & Giroux.

Taylor, Theodore. 1969. *The Cay*. New York: Delacorte Press.

Thompson, Gare. 2003. *Who Was Helen Keller?* New York: Grosset & Dunlap.

Uhlberg, Myron. 2003. *The Printer*. Atlanta: Peachtree.

Van Allsburg, Chris. 1986. *The Stranger*. Boston: Houghton Mifflin.

———. 1988. *Two Bad Ants*. Boston: Houghton Mifflin.

———. 1993. *The Sweetest Fig*. Boston: Houghton Mifflin.

Wells, Ruth. 1992. *A to Zen: A Book About Japanese Culture*. Saxonville, MA: Picture Books Studio.

White, E. B. 1952. *Charlotte's Web*. New York: HarperCollins.

Wiesner, David. 2001. *The Three Pigs*. New York: Clarion Books.

Willems, Mo. 2003. *Don't Let the Pigeon Drive the Bus*. New York: Hyperion Books for Children.

———. 2004. *The Pigeon Finds a Hotdog*. New York: Hyperion Books for Children.

———. 2005. *Leonardo, the Terrible Monster*. New York: Hyperion Books for Children.

Willis, Jeanne. 2004. *Shhh!* New York: Hyperion.

Winter, Jonah. 1991. *Diego*. New York: Random House.

Woodson, Jacqueline. 2001. *The Other Side*. New York: Putnam.

———. 2005. *Show Way*. New York: Putnam.

Yolen, Jane. 1992a. *Encounter*. Orlando: Harcourt Brace.

———. 1992b. *Letting Swift River Go*. Boston: Little, Brown and Company.

———. 2003. *Roanoke: The Lost Colony: An Unsolved Mystery from History*. New York: Simon & Schuster Books for Young Readers.

Young, Ed. 2005. *Beyond the Great Mountains: A Visual Poem About China*. San Francisco, CA: Chronicle Books.

Zweibel, Alan. 2005. *Our Tree Named Steve*. New York: G.P. Putnam's Sons.

RECOMMENDED CHILDREN'S
LITERATURE

Student Magazines

Cobblestone Publications: www.cobblestonepub.com

Kids Discover Magazine: www.kidsdisover.com

National Geographic Explorer:
www.magma.nationalgeographic.com/ngexplorer/

National Geographic Kids: www.nationalgeographic.com/ngkids/

Sports Illustrated for Kids: www.sikids.com/

Time for Kids: www.timeforkids.com

References

Allington, Richard. 2005. *What Really Matters for Struggling Readers: Designing Research-Based Programs* (2nd ed.). Upper Saddle River, NJ: Pearson.

Anderson, Carl. 2005. *Assessing Writers*. Portsmouth, NH: Heinemann.

Calkins, Lucy McCormick. 2001a. *The Art of Teaching Reading*. New York: Longman.

————. 1994. *The Art of Teaching Writing*. Portsmouth, NH: Heinemann.

Chicago Manual of Style (14th ed.). 2003. Chicago: University of Chicago Press.

Clay, Marie. 1994. *Becoming Literate*. Heinemann: Portsmouth, NH.

————. 2002. *An Observation Survey of Early Literacy Achievement*. Portsmouth, NH: Heinemann.

Duckett, Peter. 2002. New Insights: Eye Fixations and the Reading Process. *Talking Points, 13*(2).

Ferreiro, R., and A. Teberosky. 1982. *Literacy Before Schooling* (K. Goodman Castro, Trans.). Exeter, NH: Heinemann. [Original work published 1979.]

Fisher, Bobbi, and Emily Medvic. 2000. *Perspectives on Shared Reading*. Portsmouth, NH: Heinemann.

Fountas, Irene, and Gay Su Pinnell. 1996. *Guided Reading: Good First Teaching for All Children*. Portsmouth, NH: Heinemann.

————. 2001. *Guiding Readers and Writers (Grades 3–6)*. Portsmouth, NH: Heinemann.

Fox, Mem. 2001. *Reading Magic*. New York: Harcourt.

Gollasch, F. V. (Ed.). 1982. *Language & Literacy: The Selected Writings of Kenneth S. Goodman. Vol. I: Process, Theory, Research*. Boston & London: Routledge & Kegan Paul.

Goodman, Kenneth, Lois Bird, and Yetta Goodman. 1991. *Whole Language Catalog*. Santa Rosa, CA: American School Publishers.

Goodman, Yetta, Dorothy Watson, and Carolyn Burke. 1996. *Retrospective Miscue Analysis: Revaluing Readers and Reading*. Katonah, NY: R. C. Owen Publishers.

———. 2005. *Reading Miscue Inventory*. Katonah, NY: Richard C. Owen Publishers.

Graves, Donald. 1994. *A Fresh Look at Writing*. Portsmouth, NH: Heinemann.

Hahn, Mary Lee. 2000. *Reconsidering Read-aloud*. Portland, ME: Stenhouse.

Harvey, Stephanie, and Anne Goudvis. 2000. *Strategies That Work*. Portland, ME: Stenhouse.

Holdaway, Don. 1979. *The Foundations of Literacy*. Portsmouth, NH: Heinemann.

Kamii, Constance, Roberta Long, Maryann Manning, and Gary Manning. 1990. Spelling in Kindergarten: A Constructivist Analysis Comparing Spanish-Speaking and English-Speaking Children. *Journal of Research in Childhood Education, 4,* 91–97.

Kamii, Constance, and Maryann Manning. 2002. Phonemic Awareness & Beginning Reading and Writing. *Journal of Research in Childhood Education, 17*(2).

Leslie, Lauren, and JoAnne Caldwell. 2006. *Qualitative Reading Inventory* (4th ed.). Upper Saddle River, NJ: Allyn & Bacon.

Moore, Rita, and Carol Gillis. 2005. *Reading Conversations: Retrospective Miscue Analysis for Struggling Readers 412*. Portsmouth, NH: Heinemann.

Newkirk, Thomas. *Misreading Masculinity: Boys, Literacy and Popular Culture*. Portsmouth, NH: Heinemann.

Owocki, Gretchen, and Yetta Goodman. 2002. *Kidwatching: Documenting Children's Literacy Development*. Portsmouth, NH: Heinemann.

Peterson, Ralph. 1992. *Life in a Crowded Place*. Portsmouth, NH: Heinemann.

Smith, Frank. 1988. *Understanding Reading: A Psycholinguistic Analysis of Reading and Learning to Read* (4th ed.). Hillsdale, NY: Lawrence Erlbaum.

STAR Reading. 2006. Wisconsin Rapids, WI: Renaissance Learning Inc.

Terban, Marvin. 1998. *Scholastic Dictionary of Idioms*. New York: Scholastic.

Weaver, Constance. 2002. *The Reading Process*. Portsmouth, NH: Heinemann.

Wilde, Sandra. 1996. *Notes from a Kidwatcher: Selected Writings of Yetta M. Goodman*. Portsmouth, NH: Heinemann.

———. 2000. *Miscue Analysis Made Easy: Building on Student Strengths*. Portsmouth, NH: Heinemann.

Index